Macmillan/McGraw-Hill

Read-Aloud Anthology

Social Studies • Grade

- **Advertisements**
- **Biographies and Autobiographies**
- **Fiction and Nonfiction Selections**
- **Historical Fiction**
- **Journals**
- **Legends and Folk Tales**
- **Plays**
- **Poems**
- **Songs**

Macmillan McGraw-Hill

New York   Farmington

Acknowledgments

"The Buffalo Go" from AMERICAN INDIAN MYTHOLOGY by Alice Marriot and Carol K. Rachlin. © 1968 by Alice Marriot and Carol K. Rachlin. HarperCollins Publishers, New York.

HEARTLAND by Diane Siebert. © 1989 by Diane Siebert. Illustration © 1989 by Wendell Minor. HarperCollins Publishers, New York.

SIERRA by Diane Siebert. © 1991 by Diane Siebert. Illustration © 1991 by Wendell Minor. HarperCollins Publishers, New York.

"Knoxville, Tennessee" from BLACK FEELING BLACK TALK BLACK JUDGEMENT by Nikki Giovanni. ©1968 by Nikki Giovanni.

Excerpt from KATE HEADS WEST by Pat Brisson. Text © 1990 by Pat Brisson. Bradbury Press, an affiliate of Macmillan, Inc.

(continued on page 112)

Macmillan/McGraw-Hill

*A Division of The **McGraw·Hill** Companies*

Published by Macmillan/McGraw-Hill, of McGraw-Hill Education, a division of The McGraw-Hill Companies, Inc. Two Penn Plaza, New York, New York 10121.

TABLE OF *Contents*

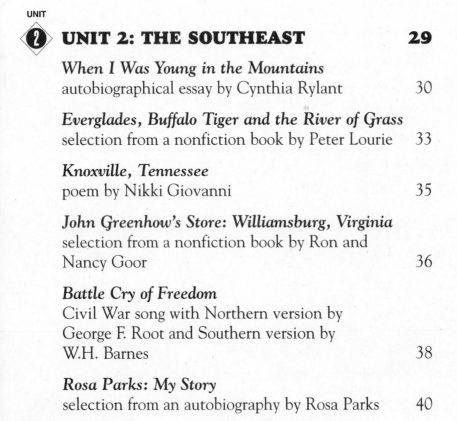

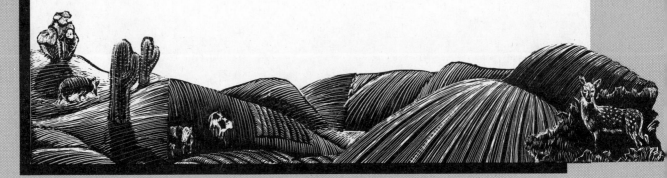

UNIT

5

UNIT 5: THE MOUNTAIN STATES

83

The readings in *Macmillan/McGraw-Hill Social Studies Anthology* have been carefully selected to enhance social studies concepts and to provide enjoyable and worthwhile reading experiences for students. All readers bring to the reading experience their own backgrounds and prior knowledge. Exposing students to a variety of viewpoints while encouraging them to question and ponder what they read will help them to become critical readers and thoughtful citizens.

The readings include **primary sources, secondary sources,** and **literature.** These fall into several categories, including:

- songs
- official documents
- oral histories
- posters
- diaries and journals
- photographs and graphics
- personal recollections

- poems
- folk tales
- letters
- autobiographies and biographies
- newspaper articles
- fiction and nonfiction
- speeches

The readings offer you a unique teaching tool. The following suggestions will help your students use the readings to build and extend their knowledge of social studies as well as to sharpen their analytical skills.

PRIMARY AND SECONDARY SOURCES

A **primary source** is something that comes from the time that is being studied. Primary sources include such things as official documents of the time, diaries and journals, letters, newspaper articles and advertisements, photographs, and oral histories. A **secondary source** is an account of the past written by someone who was not an eyewitness to those events. Remind students of the difference between primary and secondary sources. Point out that primary sources give historians valuable clues from the past because they provide firsthand information about a certain time or event. Primary sources let the reader see how people lived, felt, and thought.

However, primary sources express the view of only one person. Thus, it is important for students to understand the point of view of the writer and to find out all that they can about his or her background to decide whether the writer is credible, or believable. Secondary sources often compare and analyze different points of view and give a broader view of the event. Once again, however, it is important for students to understand the writer's point of view and analyze his or her credentials.

Suggest to students that, when they read primary and secondary sources, they ask themselves these questions:

- Who created the source?
- Can the writer be believed?
- Does the writer have expert knowledge of the subject?
- Does the writer have a reason to describe the events in a certain way?
- Does the writer have a reputation for being accurate?

You may wish to encourage students to think about the following as they read some of the various sources:

Autobiographies　What role did the subject of the autobiography play in history? Did the person live during a critical time in history? How was the person influenced by the time in which he or she lived?

Diaries and Journals　Was the diary or journal originally written to be shared with the public? Was it commissioned by a government official, such as the Columbus log was?

Speeches　Was the intent of the speech to persuade the audience to adopt a particular point of view or was the speech merely informative?

Interviews　Who is the person being interviewed? What is his or her point of view?

Advertisements　What is the purpose of the advertisement? Does it make any statements about the product that seem questionable? If so, how could you check them out?

LITERATURE

In social studies, literature is used to motivate and instruct. It also plays a large role in assisting students to understand their cultural heritage and the cultural heritage of others. For example, the folk tales included in the *Our Country's Regions Anthology*, such as "The Buffalo Go" from the Kiowa culture, were chosen to offer students glimpses of the wisdom various cultures deem important to impart. The songs, stories, and poetry of different cultures offer students opportunities to compare and contrast and hence understand aspects of cultural identity. Nonfiction selections, such as *Once a Wolf*, give students opportunities to read informational text that applies to current historical real-life issues.

In *Our Country's Regions* you will be reading about many different people, places, and times. This Anthology, or collection of documents created by different people, will make the information in your textbook come alive in a special way. The Anthology includes stories, songs, poems, diaries, interviews, letters, plays, and old advertisements and posters. As you read and study these documents, you will be able to see, feel, and hear what it is like to live in other places. Your Anthology will even take you back into the past and help you feel what it was like to live in other times! The selections in your Anthology will help you to better understand life in diverse regions of the United States, both past and present.

TEXTBOOK LINK •
Tells you which chapter and lesson in your textbook the document is linked to

INTRODUCTION •
Gives you background information about the selection and tells you what kind of document it is. Is it fiction or nonfiction? Is it a poem or a song? The introduction also asks you a question to think about as you read the document.

DEFINITIONS •
Gives you the meanings of difficult words

CONCLUSION •
Provides additional information and asks you to think further about the selection

SOURCE •
Tells you where the selection came from

Use with introduction

I Hear America Singing

by Walt Whitman, 1856

Walt Whitman was a schoolteacher, a nurse in the Civil War, a newspaper reporter, a clerk for the United States government, and also a famous American poet! Whitman's poems celebrated the "common man" in America—regular people like workers and parents and immigrants. Who are the Americans he hears singing in "I Hear America Singing"?

I hear America singing, the varied carols I hear,
Those of mechanics, each one singing his as it should be
   blithe and strong,
The carpenter singing his as he measures his plank or
   beam,
The **mason** singing his as he makes ready for work, or
   leaves off work,
The boatman singing what belongs to him in his boat, the
   deck-hand singing on the steamboat deck,
The shoemaker singing as he sits on his bench, the hatter
   singing as he stands,
The wood-cutter's song, the **ploughboy**'s on his way in the
   morning or at noon intermission or at sundown,
The delicious singing of the mother, or of the young wife
   at work, or of the girl sewing or washing,
Each singing what belongs to him or her and to none else,
The day what belongs to the day—at night the party of
   young fellows, **robust**, friendly,
Singing with open mouths their strong **melodious** songs.

blithe: happy

mason: someone who builds with stone

ploughboy: boy who plows fields on a farm

robust: strong, healthy
melodious: tuneful

Walt Whitman heard many of the different voices that make America sing. On the next page you will read about one person who felt his voice had not been heard.

Source: Walt Whitman, *Leaves of Grass.* Brooklyn, NY: Fowler and Wells, 1856.

8

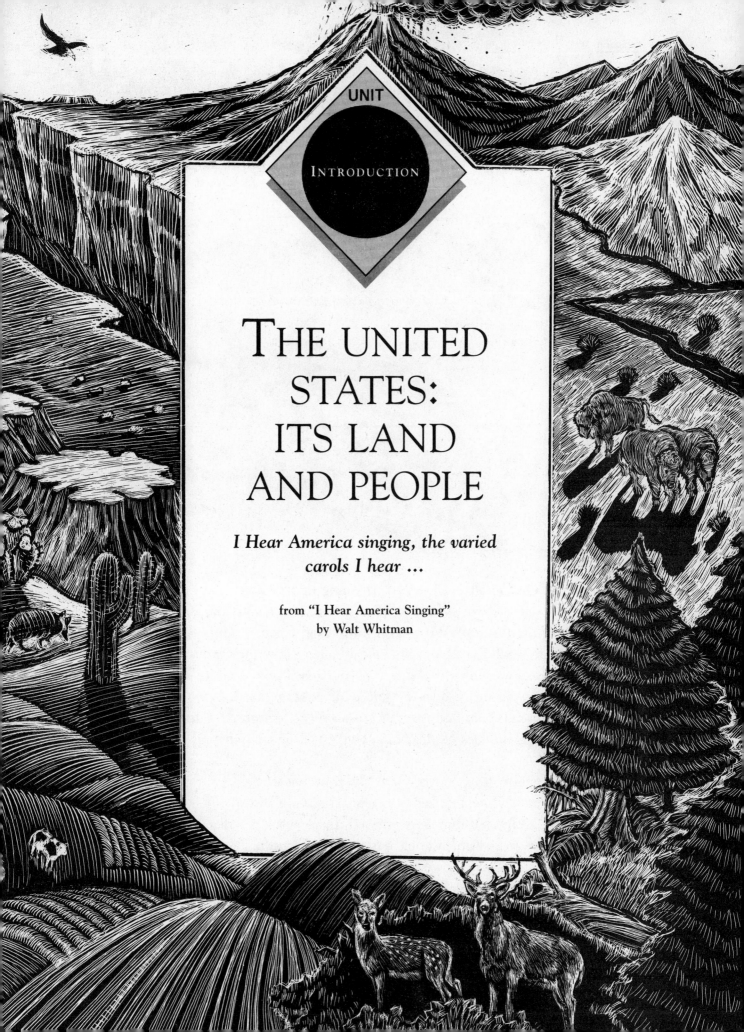

THE UNITED STATES: ITS LAND AND PEOPLE

I Hear America singing, the varied carols I hear ...

from "I Hear America Singing"
by Walt Whitman

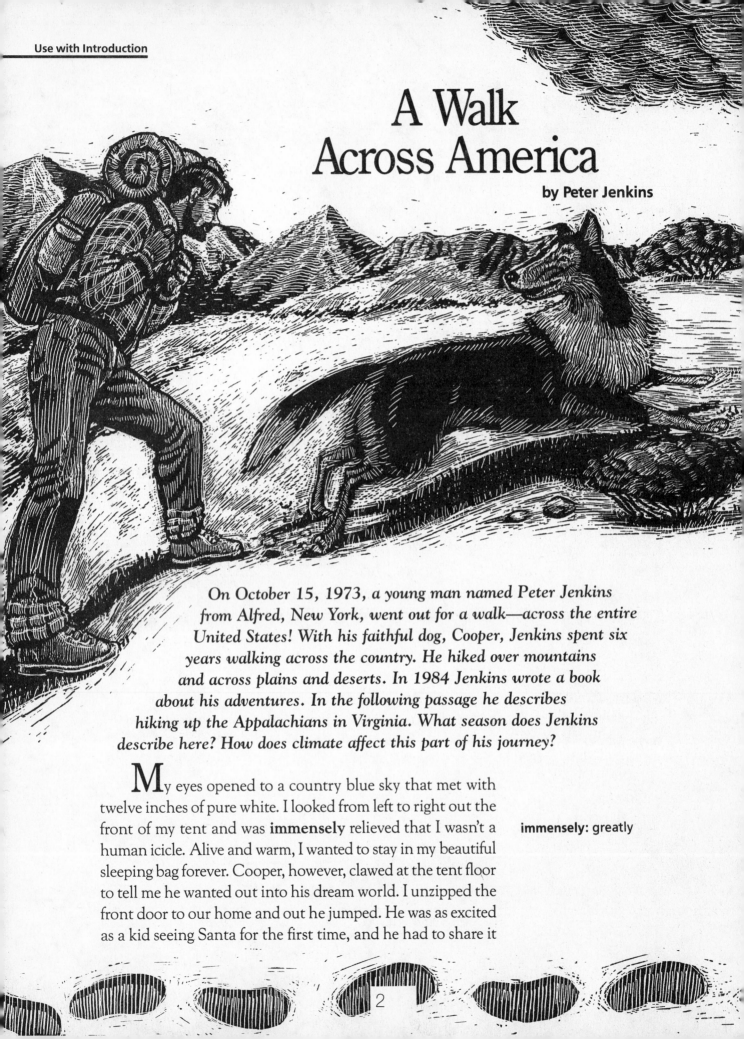

A Walk Across America

by Peter Jenkins

On October 15, 1973, a young man named Peter Jenkins from Alfred, New York, went out for a walk—across the entire United States! With his faithful dog, Cooper, Jenkins spent six years walking across the country. He hiked over mountains and across plains and deserts. In 1984 Jenkins wrote a book about his adventures. In the following passage he describes hiking up the Appalachians in Virginia. What season does Jenkins describe here? How does climate affect this part of his journey?

My eyes opened to a country blue sky that met with twelve inches of pure white. I looked from left to right out the front of my tent and was **immensely** relieved that I wasn't a human icicle. Alive and warm, I wanted to stay in my beautiful sleeping bag forever. Cooper, however, clawed at the tent floor to tell me he wanted out into his dream world. I unzipped the front door to our home and out he jumped. He was as excited as a kid seeing Santa for the first time, and he had to share it

immensely: greatly

with someone. Of course, that unlucky person was me. After a few minutes of bounding through the **pristine** powder, he crashed into the tent covered with snow and lovingly rolled over on me.

Seeing that he was making me fighting mad, he then licked my face with his bad morning breath, strong enough to **singe** my red beard. I tried desperately to crawl deeper into the bag and escape his snowy joy. Too excited to notice, he left the tent. I closed my eyes to get a little more sleep. No sooner had I relaxed when coo-coo Cooper got the cord that held up the front of the tent in his mouth and yanked the tent down with a mighty pull.

Red with rage, I shot out of the sleeping bag far enough to reach outside from under the fallen door into the snow. With both strong hands, I molded a snowball as hard as I could and when teasing Cooper came back to the front, I threw it hard, hoping to hit him in the head. Oh! I was mad! To him that snowball was more fun than baseball so from that day on, Cooper started our winter wake-up, warm-up tradition.

Inching my way far enough out of the cocoonlike bag, I sat up and put on my fluffy down jacket. Then I reached down in the bottom of the six-foot-long sleeping bag and pulled out a variety of crumpled clothes that I left there through the night to keep them warm. My **wadded-up** pants went on, ever so carefully, making sure my body wasn't out of the cozy bag before the warm pants covered the bare spots. With my body all covered, I painfully crawled out of the motherly sleeping blanket and rammed my perfume-producing white socks over my chilly feet. The only thing left to do before we could hit the road was to put on my frosted new boots. The sweat from the day before had **condensed** on the inside of the boots and turned to ice. First my right foot was frozen awake and then my left; it was a battle between the **frigid** frost and the warmth of my feet. My feet won and the stiffened boots stayed on for another traveling day. With that done, I then edged out into the world.

Instead of a steaming cup of coffee, my wake-up **tonic** was taking down the tent. This morning the back end of the tent sagged with six inches of new snow. The front end had already come down with Cooper's pranks, so taking off the rain fly was harder than usual. As I bent slowly to untie the cords from the tent stakes, I heard a fluffy charge from behind. Before I could

pristine: untouched

singe: burn

wadded-up: rolled-up

condensed: formed into drops

frigid: freezing

tonic: medicine

turn around, Cooper, the muscle-bound elf, was in the air. The next time I saw him he was on top of me. Both of us flattened the once sturdy tent, and there I lay crunched. He was so excited he barked in **hyper** screams. On the rebound, he was off again, darting through the snow as beautifully as a swimming seal.

Again, I reached down into the deep snow and made another snowball. This time I threw it as hard as a pitcher in the World Series and bouncing Cooper caught it in his mouth. Then he trotted over to me and dropped the shattered pieces of the snowball into my hand and ran back into the white field. At about fifty feet he turned around, wagged his tail and barked the way he always did when we used to play throw-the-stick. Shaking my head, I melted. I just couldn't stay mad at this happy dog who only wanted to play. My **irresistible** friend brought, for the thousandth time, a smile like all the sunshine to my face. We played throw-the-snowball-and-run for at least an hour.

The sun was high overhead by the time everything was packed up and ready to go. Back on the road, all I wanted to do was get to North Carolina. It looked only four or five days away, and North Carolina sounded much warmer than West Virginia or Virginia. What slowed us down more than I had expected was all the **continuously** curving roads. On the maps, they looked so straight. Another thing that the maps never told me was that these roads often decided to go up a mountain for four, five, or ten miles at a time. Only a few curves would give some kind of slight relief. For two days crossing through the Jefferson National Forest, we wound our way up and down and up and down through the blowing snow. The farther we went, the more **desolate** and lonely it became. People and stores were almost **extinct**, and it really got bad when we took a left on Highway 16 past Tazewell, Virginia.

We walked over mountains as high as 4,705 feet [1,434 m], weakened by lack of food. It seemed that in this draining cold I could never get enough to eat, even if there had been a store every five miles. We were lucky if we came upon one every fifteen. Then came the mountain that almost made me give up.

We camped early because that mountain stood before us and I knew that this late in the day I shouldn't even try it. I hiked through some bare fields to the top of a wooded hill, set

hyper: excited

irresistible: charming

continuously: without stopping

desolate: empty
extinct: disappeared

up the tent, crawled in, and fell asleep. Cooper was in no mood for play, and he too went to sleep before it was dark.

The morning dawned much too early and we arose in slow motion. Even happy Cooper seemed **lethargic**. He moved at a stumble, like a black bear just waking up from **hibernation**. The whole day was darkened by the gray-black storm clouds blowing in from the west. I took the frosted tent down and we walked down a stubby, cut-over field to the road. There were no houses or stores in sight, so we walked as our shrinking stomachs started burning what little fat we had for fuel. Before us were miles of "Man-eater Mountain." Stubbornly, we started up and went up, and up, and up. Every mile or two I would slow down to a snail's pace because slowing down was the only way I could rest. If I sat down in the warmth-sucking snow, I was afraid I might fall sleep.

I fought **depression**. Our enemy became the mountain, and Route 16 became the way to win. Finally I could see it! One mountaintop higher than all the rest and maybe, just maybe, that was the top of Man-eater Mountain. My damp, wrinkled map told me that if I could struggle to the top, I would be able to coast down to the town of Chattam Hill, Virginia, population 58, and please, . . . an **oasis**? I hadn't seen anything human for at least fifteen desolate miles.

I pushed and pushed my aching self and called forth all of my **waning** stores of energy. One hundred feet from me and three hundred from Cooper was the top of Man-eater Mountain. We made it! **Hysterically** I called Cooper.

Screaming, "Cooper! There's the top!" Something in the tone of my holler made Coops run and a few sprinting minutes later we were there. It didn't matter that "there" was in the middle of nowhere: we had made it to the top.

lethargic: sleepy

hibernation: a long winter sleep

depression: sadness

oasis: safe resting spot

waning: lessening

hysterically: with a lot of emotion

Jenkins made it across the Appalachians. He also made it across the Great Plains and over the Rocky Mountains, finally reaching the Pacific Ocean in 1979—six years after he first set off. In his remarkable journey, Jenkins walked almost 5,000 miles (8,045 km).

Source: Peter Jenkins, *A Walk Across America*. Carmel, NY: Guidepost Publishing Company, 1979.

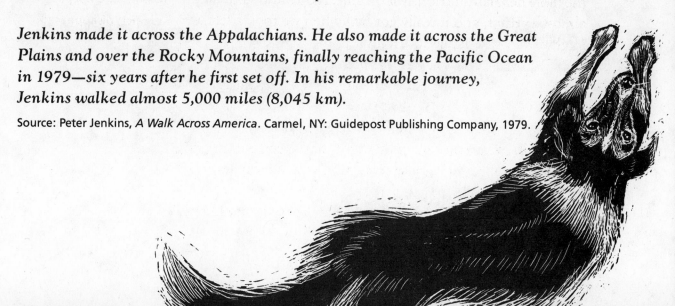

ROLL ON, COLUMBIA

by Woody Guthrie

There are many songs that describe the beauty of this country's rivers, but this is one of the few that describes how we use our rivers for electric power. In the late 1930s, many people in this country did not have electricity. The United States government started a program that helped bring hydroelectric power to the western United States. Woody Guthrie, a famous folk singer, wrote this song to celebrate the Columbia River. What does Guthrie mean when he says, "Your power is turning our darkness to dawn"?

Words by Woody Guthrie

Music based on "Goodnight Irene"
by Huddie Ledbetter and John Lomax

1. Green Doug - las fir where the wa - ters cut through,
2. Oth - er big riv - ers add power to you,

Down her wild moun - tains and can - yons she flew.
Yak - i - ma, Snake, and the Klick - i - tat, too.

Ca - na - di - an North - west to the o - cean so blue,
— Sand - y, Wil - lam - ette, and the Hood Riv - er, too,

Roll on, Co - lum - bia, roll on.

Refrain

Roll on, Co - lum - bia, roll on. Roll on, Co -

lum - bia, roll on. Your pow - er is turn - ing our

dark - ness to dawn, Roll on, Co - lum - bia, roll on.

Source: Woody Guthrie, *Roll On, Columbia*. New York: Ludlow Music, Inc. 1936.

7

I Hear America Singing

by Walt Whitman, 1856

Walt Whitman was a schoolteacher, a nurse in the Civil War, a newspaper reporter, a clerk for the United States government, and also a famous American poet! Whitman's poems celebrated the "common man" in America—regular people like workers and parents and immigrants. Who are the Americans he hears singing in "I Hear America Singing"?

I hear America singing, the varied carols I hear,
Those of mechanics, each one singing his as it should be
   blithe and strong,
The carpenter singing his as he measures his plank or
   beam,
The **mason** singing his as he makes ready for work, or
   leaves off work,
The boatman singing what belongs to him in his boat, the
   deck-hand singing on the steamboat deck.
The shoemaker singing as he sits on his bench, the hatter
   singing as he stands,
The wood-cutter's song, the **ploughboy**'s on his way in the
   morning or at noon intermission or at sundown,
The delicious singing of the mother, or of the young wife
   at work, or of the girl sewing or washing,
Each singing what belongs to him or her and to none else,
The day what belongs to the day—at night the party of
   young fellows, **robust**, friendly,
Singing with open mouths their strong **melodious** songs.

blithe: happy

mason: someone who builds with stone

ploughboy: boy who plows fields on a farm

robust: strong, healthy
melodious: tuneful

Walt Whitman heard many of the different voices that make America sing. On the next page you will read about one person who felt his voice had not been heard.

Source: Walt Whitman, *Leaves of Grass*. Brooklyn, NY: Fowler and Wells, 1856.

I, Too

by Langston Hughes, 1925

Langston Hughes was born in Joplin, Missouri, in 1902, ten years after poet Walt Whitman's death. Hughes grew up admiring Whitman's poetry about ordinary people. However, Hughes felt that one group's "songs" were not being heard: African Americans. So in 1925 Hughes sat down and wrote his own poem, "I, Too." How would you compare Walt Whitman's and Langston Hughes's views of America?

I, too, sing America.
I am the darker brother.
They send me to eat in the kitchen
When company comes,
But I laugh,
And eat well,
And grow strong.
Tomorrow,
I'll be at the table
When company comes.
Nobody'll dare
Say to me,
"Eat in the kitchen,"
Then.
Besides,
They'll see how beautiful I am
And be ashamed—
I, too, am America.

Langston Hughes's poem became as famous as Walt Whitman's. But many people had to work for civil rights to make Hughes's hope for "tomorrow" come true.

Source: Langston Hughes, *Collected Poems* by Langston Hughes. New York: Alfred A. Knopf, 1994.

SYMBOLS OF THE ★★★★ NATION

Why do you think symbols are important? If you live in California or in New York, in Texas or in Minnesota, you may have very different ways of life. But our country's symbols remind us that the 50 states are united as one nation. What does each symbol stand for?

Statue of Liberty

The Statue of Liberty in New York City's harbor has been a symbol of hope and opportunity for the millions of immigrants who saw "Miss Liberty" from their boats as they arrived in the United States. Completed in 1886, it remains a symbol of freedom and liberty for people everywhere.

United States Flag

The 13 stripes represent the 13 original states. The 50 stars represent each state today. As our country has grown, our flag has changed. At least ten different flags have represented our country since the American Revolution. The present flag has been our national symbol since 1960, when Hawaii became the fiftieth state. Every state has its own flag as well. What does your state flag look like?

Liberty Bell

Like the Statue of Liberty, the Liberty Bell is a symbol of freedom. It hung in Independence Hall in Philadelphia where the Declaration of Independence and the United States Constitution were written. It rang on July 4, 1776, to celebrate our first Independence Day.

Great Seal of the United States

Does this seal look familiar? You see it every time you look at a $1 bill. Designed over 200 years ago, the Great Seal of the United States is also found on many documents signed by the President. The American bald eagle is in the center. In one claw is an olive branch, symbolizing peace. In the other are 13 arrows, representing the strength of the 13 original states. The words *E Pluribus Unum* are Latin for "out of many, one." Out of many people, and many states, one united country is formed.

These are just some of the symbols that represent our country and our government. Can you think of any others? Suppose you had to design a symbol for your state. What ideas would you consider?

THE SOUTHWEST

*The bottom of the loom
represents the earth and the top
is the sky. The strings that
fasten the loom to the frame
represent lightning. The warp
represents the falling rain.*

From *Songs From the Loom*
by Monty Roessel

Grand Canyon East: From the Air

by Myra Cohn Livingston

The Grand Canyon, in northern Arizona, is 217 miles long, and in some places up to 18 miles wide. It can also be more than a mile deep! What do you think the Grand Canyon would look like from the window of a helicopter or an airplane? In this poem Myra Cohn Livingston gives her answer to that question. What does she compare the canyon to?

> Red rocks,
> layer after
> layer, rise up from the
> bottom of the Grand Canyon, like
> walls of
>
> old red
> brick apartment
> buildings; shattered windows
> glinting in sunlight; faded paint
> peeling.

Do you get the sense that the poet is starting at the bottom of the canyon and rising up? Why or why not? What about the Grand Canyon do you think she compares to "shattered windows"? What makes her think of "faded paint peeling"? How might the images be different if she had described the Grand Canyon "from the ground"?

Source: Myra Cohn Livingston, *Remembering and other poems*. New York: Macmillan Publishing Co., 1989.

Kate Heads West

by Pat Brisson

In Pat Brisson's story, Kate Heads West, Kate is invited to join her best friend Lucy on her family's vacation. Lucy's family is going to tour the Southwest by car. Kate and Lucy learn a lot about the Southwest and have a great time. You can learn about their trip by reading some of the postcards Kate sends back to her friends and family in New Jersey. Which places would you want to visit if you were a tourist in the Southwest?

August 6, Fort Worth, Texas
Dear Buster and Bruno,

I hope Brian's keeping your bowl nice and clean like he promised he would. If he threatens to flush you down the toilet, tell him I won't give him the **genuine** cowboy hat I bought for him at the rodeo last night in Fort Worth.

genuine: real

My favorite part of the rodeo was the cowgirls racing their horses around barrels in big figure eights. They went around the corners so fast it looked like the horses would fall right over. Lucy and I would probably be world champion barrel-racers if we lived in Texas and owned horses.

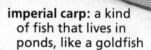

Yesterday afternoon we went to a Japanese garden. It was very quiet and peaceful there. Lucy's mom told us the Meditation Garden is just like one she's been to at a temple in Kyoto, Japan. She said it's nice to find a little bit of Japan in Texas. And there were beautiful **imperial carp** swimming in the pools there which reminded me of you.

imperial carp: a kind of fish that lives in ponds, like a goldfish

Your favorite owner,

Kate

P.S. Tell Mom and Dad not to worry—I'm being really polite.

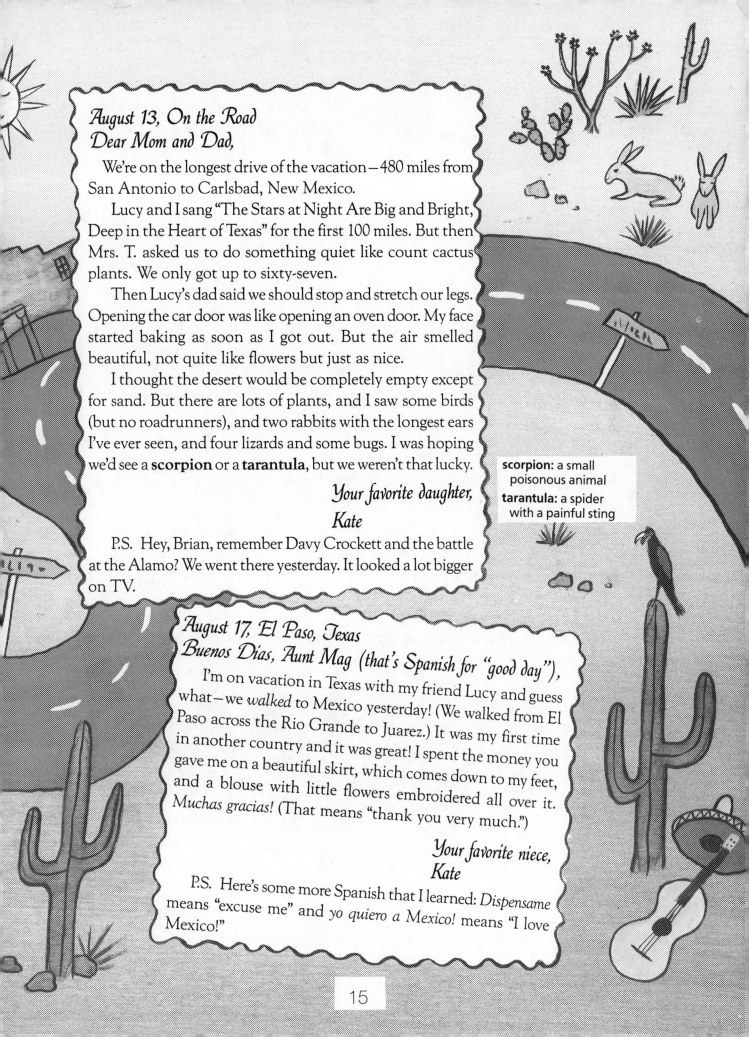

August 13, On the Road
Dear Mom and Dad,

We're on the longest drive of the vacation—480 miles from San Antonio to Carlsbad, New Mexico.

Lucy and I sang "The Stars at Night Are Big and Bright, Deep in the Heart of Texas" for the first 100 miles. But then Mrs. T. asked us to do something quiet like count cactus plants. We only got up to sixty-seven.

Then Lucy's dad said we should stop and stretch our legs. Opening the car door was like opening an oven door. My face started baking as soon as I got out. But the air smelled beautiful, not quite like flowers but just as nice.

I thought the desert would be completely empty except for sand. But there are lots of plants, and I saw some birds (but no roadrunners), and two rabbits with the longest ears I've ever seen, and four lizards and some bugs. I was hoping we'd see a **scorpion** or a **tarantula**, but we weren't that lucky.

> *Your favorite daughter,*
> *Kate*

P.S. Hey, Brian, remember Davy Crockett and the battle at the Alamo? We went there yesterday. It looked a lot bigger on TV.

scorpion: a small poisonous animal
tarantula: a spider with a painful sting

August 17, El Paso, Texas
Buenos Días, Aunt Mag (that's Spanish for "good day"),

I'm on vacation in Texas with my friend Lucy and guess what—we *walked* to Mexico yesterday! (We walked from El Paso across the Rio Grande to Juarez.) It was my first time in another country and it was great! I spent the money you gave me on a beautiful skirt, which comes down to my feet, and a blouse with little flowers embroidered all over it. *Muchas gracias!* (That means "thank you very much.")

> *Your favorite niece,*
> *Kate*

P.S. Here's some more Spanish that I learned: *Dispensame* means "excuse me" and *yo quiero a Mexico!* means "I love Mexico!"

August 18, Buckhorn, New Mexico
Dear Mrs. Heath,

How are things at the library? We visited the Gila Cliff Dwellings National Monument today. We had to climb a narrow trail to get there, and one spot was perfect for hearing your echo from the opposite wall of the canyon. Lucy and I yelled our names to see how many echoes we could get back. (Lucy got six, but I got seven.)

Anyway, the cliff dwellings are stone buildings built right into the side of the cliff. They are about a thousand years old! The Mogollon Indians built them for protection from other tribes. I guess it worked, because they lived here for hundreds of years.

Your favorite reader,
Kate

August 23, the Petrified Forest, Arizona
Dear Brian,

We are having the *best* time! Today we went to the **Petrified** Forest. It wasn't like I expected, but it was still great. I thought there would be all these trees standing around looking like concrete. But there aren't that many trees at all and actually, they're lying around like logs. They look like marbles all melted together—swirls of red and yellow and purple and pink.

I took some great pictures of the petroglyphs (old rock carvings made by the Anasazi Indians). My favorite is a mountain lion with his claws bared and his mouth open in a terrible snarl.

Tomorrow we're going to see the Hopi Snake Dance. Mr. T. said the Hopi dance with live rattlesnakes in their mouths without getting bit. We are also going to visit a pueblo built on a mesa. Mesas are hills with steep sides and flat tops, almost like tables.

Aren't you glad you're my little brother? There's so much you can learn from me.

Your favorite sister,
Kate

petrified: changed into stone

16

August 28, Grand Canyon, Arizona
Dear Mom and Dad,

Thank you, thank you, thank you for letting me come on this trip with Lucy! I can't believe I'll be home in less than a week. We're spending these last days at the Grand Canyon before we fly back. I think they should have named it the Stupendously Gigantic Canyon because it is so unbelievably big. In some places the river is a *mile* down from where we stand—I've even seen birds flying below me. At one lookout point we looked down and saw clouds. Lucy said it was fog, but I think it's the same thing.

We learned so much here that the park ranger gave us Official Junior Ranger Badges!

Yesterday we went river rafting in another canyon. Lucy and I screamed almost the entire trip, and Mr. T. said he had to give our guide a really big tip because we probably broke his eardrums.

Your favorite daughter,
Kate

When Kate returned home at the end of the trip, she had many more stories to tell about the land, the history, and the people of the Southwest. What are some things Kate and Lucy learned about on their trip? Have you ever taken a trip to a different region of the country?

Source: Pat Brisson, *Kate Heads West*. New York: Bradbury Press, 1990.

A Geyser of Oil!

by James A. Clark and Michel T. Halbouty

This excerpt from a nonfiction book about the hill called Spindletop in Beaumont, Texas, gives an exciting account of what happened on the day that drillers there struck oil. When Patillo Higgins said that an oil deposit would be found beneath the hill, few people believed him. Some even felt sorry for Higgins when he drilled and did not find anything. But one engineer, Captain Anthony Lucas, thought Higgins was right. He leased the land and had a professional drilling crew—made up of Peck Byrd and brothers Al and Curt Hamill—drill a well on the site. The date of the crew's discovery was January 10, 1901. After it, the town would not be the same. A geyser is a natural hot spring from which steam and hot water shoot into the air after being heated underground. Later the word gusher *would be used to describe what was seen in Beaumont that day. How do you think the members of the work crew felt before, during, and after the explosion?*

On the hill the crew of three had put on the new **fishtail bit**. That done, the **drill stem** was lowered back into the hole. With the pipe down about 700 feet and Curt Hamill steering it from the double boards forty feet above the **derrick** floor, something began to happen.

Mud started to bubble up over the **rotary table**. Al and Peck backed away when suddenly the force increased and mud spurted high up the derrick. Curt, drenched with mud and **gumbo** grabbed for the ladder and slid down it to safety. All three scampered in different directions. This was a new experience for these old hands of the **Corsicana** field. As they ran, six tons of four-inch pipe came shooting up through the derrick, knocking off the **crown block**. Then the pipe leapt, like activated spaghetti, on over the top of the derrick and broke off in sections, falling around the camp like giant spikes driven into the earth.

fishtail bit: cluster of rock-cutting blades at the bottom of a drill
drill stem: longest part of the drill
derrick: framework over the oil well that supports the drill
rotary table: machinery in the derrick floor that turns the drill stem
gumbo: sticky soil
Corsicana: oil drilling town about 290 miles from Beaumont
crown block: pulley system at the top of the derrick

18

Then everything was quiet. The Hamills and Peck Byrd cautiously returned to the derrick floor. It was a **shambles**, with mud, muck and water standing a foot deep. The disgusted crew looked over the situation [and] started cleaning up the **debris**. . . .

[Suddenly, they] were interrupted by a roar like the shot of a heavy cannon. Then again the flow of mud started up through the hole, followed by a terrific column of gas. The startled crew scattered again. Peck missed his footing and tumbled headlong into the **slush pit**. Within seconds, the gas was followed by a solid flow of oil—green and heavy.

"Peck, run to the house and get the Captain," Al shouted, "while Curt and me try to figure this thing out. It looks like oil! Hurry! Hurry!"

The mud-soaked Peck Byrd ran to the Lucas home. When he got there he was out of breath and sat holding his side, panting a few minutes, before he could deliver the message to **Mrs. Lucas**.

"Get the Captain! Tell him to come right now!" Peck shouted in excitement. "Look, Mrs. Lucas, look," he said, pointing to the well. But before she could find out what had happened, Peck was off on a run back to the well.

She looked toward the hill and saw a great **plume** of black liquid spouting over the derrick. The sight was fantastic. She could not explain what had happened, but she **implored** the Captain to lose no time in getting back to the hill.

"Hurry, Anthony, something awful has happened. The well is spouting," she shouted into the telephone.

The Captain turned and fled from the store without explanation. He mounted his **gig**, as Louie Mayer watched in astonishment, and stood on the floor-boards whipping his horse as he raced out Park Street, past the **O'Brien and Carroll** homes, out Highland Avenue and past his own home without looking toward his wife, who was trying to attract his attention by waving from the porch.

The **phenomenon** was in full view now. It was frightening to the Captain. His eyes had never beheld such a sight before. Could it be oil?

When he reached the hill, Lucas' excitement was too much and the horse was too slow. At the **apex** of the hill, he

shambles: place of great disorder

debris: remains of something destroyed

slush pit: hole that holds mud needed for drilling blades

Mrs. Lucas: had encouraged her husband to continue drilling even when he was thinking of giving up

plume: shape like a large, fluffy feather

implored: begged

gig: horse-drawn carriage

O'Brien and Carroll: founding partners of the Gladys City Oil Company along with Patillo Higgins

phenomenon: extraordinary event

apex: highest point

tried to jump from the buggy and tumbled down the slope. Al Hamill saw the fall and started toward him, but the Captain rolled forward and came to his feet on a **dead run**.

dead run: very fast sprint

"Al, Al," he was shouting, "what is it? What is it?"

"Oil, Captain! Oil, every drop of it," the **jubilant** Al replied.

jubilant: joyful

Grabbing Al Hamill by the waist and swinging him around, Lucas looked up toward the gray skies and said, "Thank God. Thank God, you've done it! You've done it!"

"It came in at ten-thirty, almost an hour ago, and it has been shooting a steady six-inch stream of oil more than a hundred feet above the top of the derrick, just like it is now. I can't understand it," Al said. . . .

Captain Lucas was **exultant**. He stood under the shower of green oil, felt it, smelled it and tasted it to make certain he wasn't dreaming.

exultant: rejoicing triumphantly

Then he backed off and looked up to the top of the great plume. Oil, **shale**, and rocks were raining down. Almost to himself he whispered hoarsely, with a rising **inflection**, "A geyser of oil! A geyser of oil!"

shale: fine-grained rock formed from clay

inflection: change in voice pitch

A local farmer named Charley Ingals saw the gusher, jumped on his horse, and went riding through town, calling "Oil on the hill! Oil on the hill!" Townspeople came running out to see. Ingals was not happy about the oil ruining his farmland, though. He sold his land for $1,500—a move he would later regret. Many other local farmers, ranchers, and businesspeople became rich after the discovery of "black gold" in Beaumont. And some 40,000 people moved to the town to work in the booming oil industry. Why is oil, or petroleum, so valuable? What are some of its uses?

Source: James A. Clark and Michel T. Halbouty, *Spindletop*. New York: Random House, Inc., 1952.

Songs From the Loom
by Monty Roessel

The Southwest has long been home to the Navajo Native Americans. Like many cultures, the Navajo have used storytelling as a way to keep their culture alive over many years. The stories are passed down from one generation to the next. In this way people all over the world kept their heritage alive long before there were printed books. Today, storytelling continues as a tradition among Native Americans. In this selection the author retells the story of why the Navajo people weave. Why do you think this is an important story to the Navajo?

A long time ago, right after we **emerged** into the Fourth World—the Glittering World—there was a Holy Person named Changing Woman. She had twin boys: their names were Monster Slayer and Child Born for Water.

emerged: to come into being

The twins decide to plan a secret trip. To make sure that their mother did not hear about it, the twins only discussed their plans away from the **hogan.** One evening while they were walking, they heard a voice. They couldn't tell where it came from. Upon hearing it the fourth time, they saw a tiny hole in the ground. They both kneeled down and looked into the hole.

hogan: a dwelling made of logs and wood

All of a sudden, they were in a room with beautifully designed blankets all around them. An old woman's voice quietly said, "It is dark, my children, you shouldn't be out this late." The boys looked at her and asked her name. She told them she was Spider Woman. They told her about their secret plan, and they asked about the blankets. They had never seen anything like them before—they only knew about buckskin. They were amazed that the old Spider Woman had made them.

When they returned home, their mother asked where they had been. The boys only said they had visited an old lady who made beautiful blankets. Changing Woman was **suspicious,** but she became fascinated with the story of the weaver and didn't ask any more questions.

suspicious: mistrustful

One day, Changing Woman visited Spider Woman. She wanted to see the blankets for herself. She also wanted to learn to weave. Spider Woman agreed to teach her, with one condition. Changing Woman would have to teach other Navajo women. She agreed.

The first thing Changing Woman wanted to learn was how to make those beautiful colors and designs. Spider Woman told her the colors came from the earth. "From the east I get white, from the south I get blue, from the west I get yellow, and from the north I get black. These colors come from white shell, turquoise, abalone, and jet. But these same colors, and more, can also be made from plants.

"The designs come from the earth. Clouds, lightning, sunbeams, and mountains.

"The bottom of the loom represents the earth and the top is the sky. The strings that fasten the loom to the frame represent lightning. The **warp** represents the falling rain. This is why you must never weave during rain and lightning. You also must never sketch your rug before you start. The weaving must come from your mind and heart."

warp: a series of yarns extended lengthwise

After Spider Woman had taught Changing Woman how to weave, she gave her one last instruction. Every rug that has a border must have an opening, a small break—usually nothing more than a light-colored piece of yarn woven into the dark border that goes to the edge of the blanket. It is sort of like an escape from the middle of the blanket. "If you don't leave an opening," she said, "You will close in your life and thoughts. You will be unable to learn any more."

Then Changing Woman went away and began to teach other women what she had learned.

If you were to tell a story about your heritage, what would you say? How do you think telling your story out loud would be different from writing it down and asking someone else to read it?

Source: Monty Roessel, *Songs From the Loom.* Minneapolis: Lerner Publications Company, 1995.

Spanish Pioneers of the Southwest

by Joan Anderson

The Spanish were the first Europeans to settle in the Southwest. The following is an excerpt from a book about a Spanish settlement called El Rancho de las Golandrinas (EL RAHN choh de las goh lahn DREE nahs), near what is now Santa Fe, New Mexico. Miguel Baca is a young child in the family that lives on the ranch in the middle 1700s. The Baca family farms, raises sheep, and runs an inn for travelers. Although they are on good terms with their Pueblo neighbors, they are fighting with the nearby Navajo. Miguel's older brother, Pedro, has been taken captive in a Navajo raid. Miguel wonders about what Pedro is doing, even as he tries to take his place on the ranch. What is a day like for Miguel?

It was warm and cozy in the Bacas' *cocina*. The chili stew smelled **delectable** as the family gathered and **Abuelita** Luisa dished it up. Everyone sat quietly, exhausted but content to be slowing down from the toils of the day.

The chill of the night descended upon them. Emilio Baca built up the fire as his wife, Isabel, unrolled the blankets and sheepskins that would become their beds. Miguel's father took his place atop the fireplace, and the others huddled close to the hearth.

Miguel felt his muscles relax as his mother began to sing softly to the baby. For the first time all day, Miguel knew he was safe. Only here in the cozy *cocina* did he feel he could let his guard down. He couldn't let Papá know that he

cocina (koh-SEE nah): kitchen
delectable: delicious
Abuelita (ah bwe LEE tah): Grandma

wasn't all that brave. So on the outside, Miguel stood tall and proud, but on the inside he trembled with fear.

Dawn came early. With only a few tiny windows in the Bacas' *cocina*, it was impossible to know when the sun came up. But the *patrón* took care that the people of Golondrinas were alerted to the early hour by ringing the **hacienda's** huge iron bell.

patrón (pah TROHN): landlord, boss

hacienda (ah see EN dah): ranch house

Miguel stirred upon hearing the dull clang. One. Two. Three. Four. Five. On the fifth ring he bolted upright. Glancing about the room he saw that Papá's bed was vacant! Was he already at work? Miguel quickly rolled up his blanket, gulped down a cup of *atole*, and headed out the door.

atole (ah TOH LE): cornflour porridge

Sure enough, Papá was down by the stream near the small plot of **cultivated** farmland. Miguel ran as fast as he could, anxious to show his father that even though he wasn't as big and strong as Pedro, he was eager to work.

cultivated: prepared, tilled

"I'm here, Papá," he announced. "What shall I do?"

"Quickly, grab hold of the yoke while I secure it to their horns. These beasts want nothing of work this morning."

Miguel did as his father said, and eventually they attached the **crude** wooden plow and headed for the far end of the field. The earth was hard and dry. Miguel was always amazed that things grew in such unhealthy-looking soil.

crude: rough, homemade

"Papá," he asked, his teeth chattering in the early morning chill, "isn't it still too cold for planting?"

"It would seem so, my son," Emilio Baca answered as the **plowshare** dug into the soil and began to turn the earth. "But we must hope that the days soon become warm, as it takes many months to grow our corn and beans and wheat. Besides, **Padre** José will come to bless our fields during the **Feast of San Ysidro**. If we haven't done our work there can be no blessing, *sí?*"

plowshare: front edge or blade of plow

Padre (PAH dre): Father, priest

Feast of San Ysidro (SAHN ee SEE droh): holiday celebrating the coming of spring

"I suppose not, Papá," Miguel answered, working steadily now. It felt good to be sharing chores with someone instead of being alone tending sheep and collecting wood. Time passed quickly, and by late afternoon they were putting in the seed. Miguel felt proud of their accomplishment, especially since the *patrón* had been watching their progress from the rooftop on the hacienda. . . .

During the next few days, Miguel went about his regular chores hoping that soon the *patrón* would remember his promise and permit him to stand watch in the **torreon**.

Each morning he tossed fresh straw into the **corral** for the barn animals to eat. He fed the chickens and turkeys, milked the goats, and held the sheep steady while they were sheared.

In the afternoons, sometimes with his father, sometimes alone, he took the sheep to the nearby hills to graze. The days were long and hard, and Miguel began to wonder why there seemed to be more work this spring than in other years. Then he realized—Pedro wasn't there this year to share in all the work. . . .

[One morning] all regular chores were put aside so that the villagers could prepare for the festival. Padre José was needed in other settlements and would stay for only a day or two.

The saint maker of Golondrinas had been working day and night in anticipation of the padre's arrival. His beautiful carving of San Ysidro plowing the fields was almost complete. Miguel loved to watch as he mixed brightly colored paints from different plants and chipped away at a block of wood until the block disappeared and in its place was a magnificent figure. Tomorrow San Ysidro, the patron saint of farmers, would be carried about the hacienda on his way to the little chapel. From this spot, high above Golondrinas, he would bless and watch over the fields until harvest.

Nearby, Doña María was hunched over a bunch of dried chilis, picking out the seeds and grinding them into powder. Blue corn would be ground as well to make flour for all the tortillas that would be consumed at the fiesta. **Polonia** stood patiently beside the *hornos* waiting for the *dulces* to bake. Everyone loved the sweet-tasting bread that was made for special occasions.

Finally, it was May 15; the Feast of San Ysidro was upon them.

A procession formed and the crowd moved slowly out of the great pine gate. Carrying the statue of San Ysidro on their shoulders, they wove their way down the hillside to

torreón (toh re OHN): large tower, fort

corral: fenced-off space for animals

Polonia: a Navajo servant in Miguel's village who has adopted Spanish ways. Miguel wonders if his brother Pedro has similarly adopted Navajo ways.

hornos (OR nohs): ovens

dulces (DOOL ses): sweet, dessert breads

the precious **irrigation ditch**, around the newly planted field of crops, through the pasture, until finally they approached the chapel. They chanted as they walked.

> San Ysidro, land tiller
> Protect our crops
> From pests and storms
> San Ysidro, golden whiskered
> Pray to God
> To send us rain in torrents

Miguel watched as they placed the wooden saint gently on the altar of the tiny church. From there, San Ysidro could watch the hacienda and all of its people.

After the ceremony, the padre stood off to the side, his mind deep in thought.

"Padre," Miguel said, "already since your arrival it seems to me that the soil looks richer."

"My boy," Padre José answered, "this is good land that God has given to us to settle upon. If we care for it, taking only what we need, as our Pueblo Indian neighbors do, it will serve us with **abundance**."

abundance: plenty

Miguel looks forward to the Feast of San Ysidro and works hard to prepare for it. What role did religion play in the life of Spanish settlers in the colonial Southwest?

Source: Joan Anderson, *Spanish Pioneers of the Southwest*. New York: E.P. Dutton, 1989.

An American Cowboy Song

Many people think that "dogies" are dogs—but "dogies" is the name cowboys used for the motherless calves that strayed from the herds on the long drives from Texas to the railroads. When the cowboys drove their herds north, they sang to themselves and to each other. Sometimes, as in this song, the cowboys sang to the dogies! How does the music sound like cattle moving along?

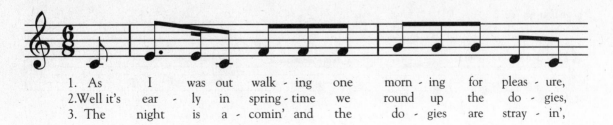

1. As I was out walk-ing one morn-ing for pleas-ure,
2. Well it's ear-ly in spring-time we round up the do-gies,
3. The night is a-comin' and the do-gies are stray-in',

I saw a young cow-boy a rid-ing a long;
We train them to fol-low and nev-er to stray;
They're far-ther from home ___ than they've been be-fore;

His hat was thrown back and his spurs were a jing-lin',
Then load the chuck wag-ons with beans and with ba-con,
Come on lit-tle do-gies, it's time to be roll-in',

And as he ap-proached he was sing-ing this song.
And as soon as there's day-light we'll be on our way.
When we get to Wy-o-ming we'll roll ___ no more.

Refrain

Whoop-ee ti-yi-yo, git a-long, lit-tle do-gies,

It's your mis-for-tune and none of my own;

Whoop-ee ti-yo-yo, git a-long, lit-tle do-gies,

For you know Wy-o-ming will be your new home.

28

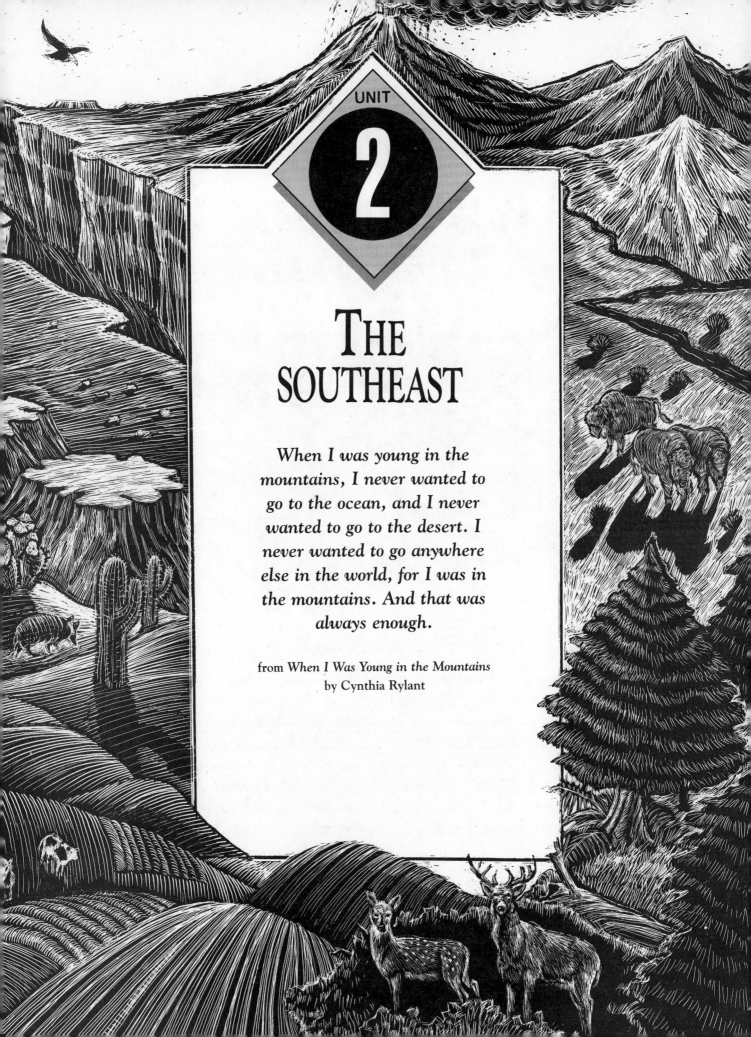

THE SOUTHEAST

When I was young in the mountains, I never wanted to go to the ocean, and I never wanted to go to the desert. I never wanted to go anywhere else in the world, for I was in the mountains. And that was always enough.

from *When I Was Young in the Mountains*
by Cynthia Rylant

When I Was Young in the Mountains

by Cynthia Rylant

Cynthia Rylant grew up in the Appalachian Mountains, in Cool Ridge, West Virginia. Her grandfather was a coal miner, and they lived in a small house with no running water. Times may have been tough, but her memories are of a simple, happy life. Rylant remembers little things with great joy, like swimming in a swimming hole and pumping water from a well. Her memories are from a different time, the 1950s. Many things have changed since the time that Rylant remembers. But life in the Appalachian Mountains is still different from life in a city. How do you think that living in the mountains affects a person's way of life?

When I was young in the mountains, Grandfather came home in the evening covered with the black dust of a coal mine. Only his lips were clean, and he used them to kiss the top of my head.

When I was young in the mountains, Grandmother spread the table with hot corn bread, pinto beans and fried okra. Later, in the middle of the night, she walked through the grass with me to the **johnny-house** and held my hand in the dark. I promised never to eat more than one serving of okra again.

When I was young in the mountains, we walked across the cow pasture and through the woods, carrying our towels. The swimming hole was dark and muddy, and we sometimes saw snakes, but we jumped in anyway. On our way home, we stopped at Mr. Crawford's for a mound of white butter. Mr. Crawford and Mrs. Crawford looked alike and always smelled of sweet milk.

When I was young in the mountains, we pumped pails of water from the well at the bottom of the hill, and heated the water to fill round tin tubs for our baths. Afterwards we stood in front of the old black stove, shivering and giggling, while Grandmother heated cocoa on top.

When I was young in the mountains, we went to church in the schoolhouse on Sundays, and sometimes walked with the **congregation** through the cow pasture to the dark swimming hole, for **baptism**. My cousin Peter was laid back into the water, and his white shirt stuck to him, and my Grandmother cried.

johnny-house: an outdoor bathroom

congregation: church group

baptism: a religious ceremony in which a person is dipped into water

When I was young in the mountains,
we listened to frogs sing at dusk and
awoke to cowbells outside our windows.
Sometimes a black snake came in the yard,
and my Grandmother would threaten it with
a hoe. If it did not leave, she used the hoe to kill
it. Four of us once **draped** a very long snake, dead
of course, across our necks for a photograph.

hoe: long tool used
for loosening soil
draped: hung

When I was young in the mountains, we sat on the porch
swing in the evenings, and Grandfather sharpened my pencils
with his pocket knife. Grandmother sometimes shelled beans
and sometimes braided my hair. The dogs lay around us, and
the stars sparkled in the sky. A bob white whistled in the forest.
Bob-bob-bob white!

When I was young in the mountains, I never wanted to go
to the ocean, and I never wanted to go the desert. I never
wanted to go anywhere else in the world, for I was in the
mountains. And that was always enough.

*Today you may swim in a pool and get your water from a faucet. But you may
also find pleasure in simple things. What are some of the things you enjoy about
your everyday life? How do you think you'll describe them to younger people
when you grow up?*

Source: Cynthia Rylant, *When I Was Young in the Mountains*. New York: E. P. Dutton, 1982.

Everglades, Buffalo Tiger and The River of Grass
by Peter Lourie

This excerpt is a true story about the writer's trip through the Florida Everglades. During his journey he relied on his guide, a Miccosukee Native American and former chief, named Buffalo Tiger. He found the Everglades to be a mysterious and dangerous place where alligators, deadly snakes, and quicksand always await visitors. As you read, imagine what it was like to travel through this swampy land with its razor-sharp sawgrass. Yet, this river of grass is also home to many kinds of birds and other wildlife whose existence is endangered in their natural habitat. What do you think the writer learns about the Everglades as a result of his trip?

The day came when I would enter the Everglades by airboat. Buffalo's assistant canoed out and disappeared among the reeds. Suddenly there was a loud roar, like the sound of an airplane revving up. From behind the bushes, where it had been anchored for safety from vandals, the big airboat moved cautiously up to the dock. And what an odd contraption this airboat was: part airplane, part boat. Buffalo stepped up to the controls and sat high above the water, where he could see over the **sawgrass.** He steered with a long stick in one hand. From his high seat he could look out at the channels and find the best route through the Glades.

sawgrass: type of grass with sharp teeth

Airboats are recent arrivals to the Glades. When Buffalo was a boy, he and his friends poled heavy **dugout canoes** made from large cypress trees. But now most of the big trees have been cut, and the remaining ones grow on private property. So there are no more dugouts, though Buffalo told me he would love to get his hands on a cypress to build another canoe.

dugout canoes: boats made by hollowing out a large log

We headed out into the Glades at top speed, following the airboat trails, which look like canals cut in the sawgrass. The 360-degree expanse of blue sky made me dizzy. Suddenly the engine died, and we sat out there alone. The wind raked through the high sawgrass. Buffalo pointed to some trees on the horizon.

"I was born right over there," he said. "Our family had six islands, what we call hammocks. We built our homes on one big hammock, which was high enough to be protected even in a hurricane. We used the other islands for farming."

Buffalo had recently cleared a field and built Miccosukee-style homes, the traditional palm-thatch *chikees*, on a nearby hammock. Someday, he said, he would take me to that favorite hammock of his.

"Could I camp there? I asked, though I was afraid he would say no.

"Perhaps one of these days, if we become friends," he said. Then he put on his ear protectors and started the engine, and away we fled over the golden grass beneath the navy blue sky. I felt free out there, the way I often feel at sea when there is nothing in sight but water.

We came shushing to a halt again. We were sitting in a patch of mud beside a wall of ten-foot-high sawgrass. I ran my hand down a blade of grass. It was three-sided and had "teeth." Buffalo pointed to the mud, explaining that alligators and snakes like to go underneath it because it is cool down there. Buffalo grabbed a long pole and poked it over the side into the mud, which he called quicksand. He told me about the danger of quicksand. If I should ever get caught in this mud, he said, I should lie down immediately and crawl the way alligators do on their bellies.

"There's a mother alligator in here right now," he said, "with her young." Buffalo poked the mud with his pole and started to call her out with a kind of croaking sound in his throat, an alligator mating call! The mother alligator finally rose to the surface **begrudgingly** and slid over the mud. She came to rest watching us.

begrudgingly: to give reluctantly

"When I was a boy out here," said Buffalo, "the alligators didn't seem so mean. But I think with all the changes and the hunting now, they are getting meaner." Buffalo's face was stern. The airboat roared into action.

A blue heron and an egret flew into the horizon. The wind seemed ever present, the way it does in a desert. We raced home in the dusk while the water lilies closed up for the night. I wondered how Buffalo and the other Miccosukees had hidden from the white men for so many years. Then I remembered that those were the days before the airboats, when the whites would have to slog through the Glades by foot or pole their boats in a swamp they knew little about.

Why is it important for people to learn as much as possible about endangered places such as the Everglades?

Source: Peter Lourie, *Everglades, Buffalo Tiger and the River of Grass.* Honesdale, PA: Boyds Mills Press, 1994.

KNOXVILLE, TENNESSEE

by Nikki Giovanni

*What do you think of when you think about summer? Perhaps you think of
vacation, swimming, baseball, and enough sunshine to be able to play outdoors
after dinner. Poet Nikki Giovanni remembers her summers in Knoxville,
Tennessee. What are some of the reasons that summer is her favorite season?*

I always like summer

best

you can eat fresh corn

from daddy's garden

and okra

and greens

and cabbage

and lots of barbecue

and buttermilk

and homemade ice cream

at the church picnic

and listen to

gospel music

outside

at the church

homecoming

and go to the mountains
  with

your grandmother

and go barefooted

and be warm

all the time

not only when you go
  to bed

and sleep

*Which season do you like best? If you wrote a poem about that season, what
things would you include?*

Source: Nikki Giovanni, *Black Feeling Black Talk Black Judgement*. New York: William Morrow &
Company, Inc., 1968.

John Greenhow's Store
Williamsburg, Virginia

by Ron and Nancy Goor

General stores were an important part of colonial life. In these shops people could buy whatever they could not make themselves. Most of these items were imported from Europe. In Williamsburg, the capital of the Virginia Colony, many items came from England. Although the colonists wanted America to be imdependent, Americans could not yet manufacture all the things they needed and wanted. On the next page you can see a photograph of John Greenhow's store from present-day "Colonial Williamsburg." The people in the photograph are actors helping visitors to understand what life was like in colonial times. What items are for sale in the store?

Stores such as John Greenhow's were stocked with **a multitude of** imported goods. You could buy your quills, ink powder and note books, Irish **linens**, fashionable buttons, smoothing irons, ready-made shirts…iron kettles, sponges, brooms, and tools for almost every occasion.

At Greenhow's you could purchase anything you might need or just enjoyed having. However you had to use ready money (Spanish or Dutch coins). Mr. Greenhow accepted no credit. A popular form of money in the Virginia colony was notes of credit made with London tobacco merchants and other kinds of promises to pay. Virginia colonists were forced to use these types of currency because England would not allow them to mint their own coins or to use English ones. Often they resorted to **barter**. A housewife might pay for a bag of sugar with a dozen eggs. When they could, townspeople bought on credit and took years to pay.

a multitude of: many

linens: household items made of cloth, such as sheets and towels

barter: trade

Other kinds of stores were also important in colonial Williamsburg. The milliner's shop offered locally-made hats and imported clothes. At the silversmith's, colonists could buy small objects like spoons or have their silver coins made into serving pieces for safer keeping. And men could always visit the wig maker's to find wigs in the latest fashion. (Women wore their hair curled.) Above you can see posters advertising shops run by two other Williamsburg craftsmen. What services do they offer?

Source: Ron and Nancy Goor, *Williamsburg: Cradle of the Revolution.* New York: Atheneum, 1994.

BATTLE CRY OF FREEDOM

Civil War Battle Song

Northern Version by George F. Root, 1861   Southern Version by W. H. Barnes, 1861

When the Civil War began in 1861, songwriters rushed to write songs for soldiers to sing. One of the most popular songs to sweep the North was George F. Root's "Battle Cry of Freedom." Union troops sang it in camp, in battle, and when marching. The tune was so catchy that Confederate troops also began singing it—but they, of course, wanted different words. So a Southerner named W. H. Barnes wrote a new version for the South. How do the two versions reveal two different perspectives?

Spirited

North: 1. Yes we'll ral - ly 'round the flag, boys, we'll
South: 1. Our _____ flag is proud - ly float-ing, On the

ral - ly once a - gain, Shout - ing the bat - tle cry of
land and on the main, Shout, shout the bat - tle cry of

Free - dom, We will ral - ly from the hill - side, we'll
Free - dom; Be - neath it oft we've con-quered, And will

gath - er from the plain, Shout - ing the bat - tle cry of Free - dom.
con - quer oft a - gain, Shout, shout the bat - tle cry of Free - dom.

Chorus

North: The Un - ion for - ev - er, Hur - rah, boys, Hur - rah!
South: Our Dix - ie for - ev - er, she's nev - er at a loss;

Down with the trai-tor, Up with the star; While we
Down with the ea-gle, Up with the cross. We'll___

ral-ly 'round the flag, boys, Ral-ly once a-gain.
ral-ly 'round the bon-ny flag, we'll ral-ly once a-gain.

1.   2.

Shout-ing the bat-tle cry of Free-dom. Free-dom.
Shout, shout the bat-tle cry of Free-dom. Free-dom.

North:

2. We are springing to the call
   Of our brothers gone before,
     Shouting the battle cry of Freedom,
   And we'll fill the vacant ranks
   With a million Free men more,
     Shouting the battle cry of Freedom.

Chorus

3. We will welcome to our numbers
   The loyal, true and brave,
     Shouting the battle cry of Freedom,
   And although he may be poor
   He shall never be a slave,
     Shouting the battle cry of Freedom.

Chorus

4. So we're springing to the call
   From the East and from the West,
     Shouting the battle cry of Freedom,
   And we'll hurl the rebel crew
   From the land we love the best,
     Shouting the battle cry of Freedom.

Chorus

South:

2. Our gallant boys have marched
   To the rolling of the drums,
     Shout, shout the battle cry of Freedom;
   And the leaders in charge
   Cry, "Come boys, come!"
     Shout, shout the battle cry of Freedom.

Chorus

3. They have laid down their lives
   On the bloody battle field,
     Shout, shout the battle cry of Freedom;
   Their motto is resistance—
   "To tyrants we'll not yield!"
     Shout, shout the battle cry of Freedom.

Chorus

4. While our boys have responded
   And to the field have gone,
     Shout, shout the battle cry of Freedom;
   Our noble women also
   Have aided them at home.
     Shout, shout the battle cry of Freedom.

Chorus

Source: Paul Glass and Louis Singer, *Singing Soldiers: A History of the Civil War in Song.*
New York: Da Capo Press, 1975.

Rosa Parks: My Story

by Rosa Parks

For many years African Americans in the South had been forced by law to sit in separate sections of trains and buses. Most blacks opposed these unfair laws, and on December 1, 1955, a woman in Montgomery, Alabama, decided to do something about them. What did Rosa Parks do? Parks tells you herself in the following selection from her autobiography. In what ways does she show courage?

When I got off from work that evening of December 1, I went to Court Square as usual to catch the Cleveland Avenue bus home. I didn't look to see who was driving when I got on, and by the time I recognized him, I had already paid my fare. It was the same driver who had put me off the bus back in 1943, twelve years earlier. He was still tall and heavy, with red, rough-looking skin. And he was still mean-looking. I didn't know if he had been on that route before—they switched the drivers around sometimes. I do know that most of the time if I saw him on a bus, I wouldn't get on it.

I saw a **vacant** seat in the middle section of the bus and took it. I didn't even question why there was a vacant seat even though there were quite a few people standing in the back. If I had thought about it at all, I would probably have figured maybe someone saw me get on and did not take the seat but left it vacant for me. There was a man sitting next to the window and two women across the aisle.

The next stop was the Empire Theater, and some whites got on. They filled up the white seats, and one man was left standing. The driver looked back at us. He said, "Let me have

vacant: empty

40

those front seats," because they were the front seats of the black section. Didn't anybody move. We just sat where we were, the four of us. Then he spoke a second time: "Y'all better **make it light** on yourselves and let me have those seats."

The man in the window seat next to me stood up, and I moved to let him pass by me, and then I looked across the aisle and saw that the two women were also standing. I moved over to the window seat. I could not see how standing up was going to "make it light" for me. The more we gave in and complied, the worse they treated us. . . .

People always say that I didn't give up my seat because I was tired, but that isn't true. I was not tired physically, or no more tired than I usually was at the end of a working day. I was not old, although some people have an image of me as being old then. I was forty-two. No, the only tired I was, was tired of giving in.

The driver of the bus saw me still sitting there, and he asked was I going to stand up. I said, "No." He said, "Well, I'm going to have you arrested." Then I said, "You may do that." These were the only words we said to each other. I didn't even know his name, which was James Blake, until we were in court together. He got out of the bus and stayed outside for a few minutes, waiting for the police.

In the 1950s African Americans were forced by law to sit separately, in the back of the bus.

41

Rosa Parks takes a seat where she chooses, one year after her historic protest which led to the end of segregation on public transportation.

As I sat there, I tried not to think about what might happen. I knew that anything was possible. I could be **manhandled** or beaten. I could be arrested. People have asked me if it occurred to me then that I could be the test case the **NAACP** had been looking for. I did not think about that at all. In fact if I had let myself think too deeply about what might happen to me, I might have gotten off the bus. But I chose to remain.

manhandled: treated roughly

NAACP: National Association for the Advancement of Colored People, an organization that works for civil rights

Rosa Parks was arrested and put into jail. Word spread quickly throughout the African American community, and people became very angry. They, too, were tired of giving in. Led by Dr. Martin Luther King, Jr., African Americans joined together and refused to ride the city buses at all. Finally, a year later, the segregation laws were changed. Rosa Parks has spent the rest of her life working for civil rights for all people. "Everyone living together in peace and harmony and love," she writes, ". . . that's the goal that we seek."

Source: Rosa Parks, *Rosa Parks: My Story.* New York: Dial Books, 1992.

UNIT

3

THE NORTHEAST

Listen, my children,
and you shall hear
Of the midnight ride
of Paul Revere.

from "Paul Revere's Ride"
by Henry Wadsworth Longfellow

FALL

by Karla Kuskin

Autumn in the Northeast is known for its colorful leaves and its cool, crisp weather. Some people say that this time of year "sharpens the senses." Which of the five senses does poet Karla Kuskin use most on her fall walk in this poem? Why do you think she describes her own clothing?

When I go walking in the fall
I stop to watch the deer.
They open up their lovely eyes
And blink
And disappear.
The rabbits hop from here
To there
And in
And out
And under
While deep within the forest heart
The black bears roar like thunder.
The chipmunks gather butternuts
And hide them in a tree
Where clever squirrels
Discover them
And laugh with squirrelish glee.
My hat is green
My jacket blue
With patches on the sleeves
And as I walk
I crunch through piles
Of red and yellow leaves.

What is autumn like where you live? Is it much like the other seasons, or is it very different? If you were to take a walk in the fall, what would you see and hear?

Source: Karla Kuskin, *Dogs and Dragons, Trees and Dreams.* New York: Harper & Row, 1980.

Blow, Ye Winds, in the Morning

The harbors and bays of New England make the Northeast a rich fishing area. At one time whales were hunted in these waters. Whale fat, or blubber, was used to make oil. Later, kerosene replaced whale fat as a source of fuel. Other ways of harvesting the resources of the sea are now more common, but songs such as this one recall the whalers who sailed out of ports like New Bedford. What other Northeastern towns are mentioned in the song? Why do you think the whalers needed to be "brave"?

Traditional
Arranged by Jerome Epstein

G/D   G

morn - ing ____ Blow, ye winds, high - O!

C   Am   Em   G/B Am/C D7   G

Clear a - way the run-ning gear and blow, boys, blow!"

2. They send you to New Bedford
that famous whaling port,
And give you to some land sharks
to board
and fit you out—singin',

Chorus

3. They tell you of the clipper ships
a-going in and out,
And say you'll take five hundred
whales,
before you're six months out—
singin',

Chorus

Source: Amy L. Cohn, ed., *From Sea to Shining Sea: A Treasury of American Folklore and Folk Songs.* New York: Scholastic, 1993.

Woodpecker and Sugar Maple
retold by Jane Louise Curry

The following Lenape tale is typical in its explanation of the natural world and the interdependence that occurs among wildlife for survival. How do Sugar Maple and Woodpecker rely on each other? Why is this relationship important in maintaining Nature's balance?

Not long after the world was made new, after the animals chose their new homes, and the trees and plants grew strong and green, Sugar Maple began to itch. Dozens of little beetles had decided to make their homes under his bark. They nibbled their way in, and tunneled in all directions. When their eggs hatched into grubs, the grubs tunneled, too. The itch was so bad that Sugar Maple moaned and swayed and twisted in torment. The dozens of beetles became hundreds, then hundreds more, and they all nibbled away busily.

"Help!" cried Sugar Maple when he could stand it no longer. "Someone—anyone—everyone—*help!*"

"You'll feel better tomorrow," Beaver called as he **bustled** by. "Keep busy. Try not to think of it."

bustled: to move in a hurry

Then Woodpecker came.

"Grubs? Under your bark?" He cocked a bright eye. "Yes I can help. So can my cousins." So he flew away, and returned with Flicker and Downey Woodpecker.

They peeled away busily at Sugar Maple's bark. They picked out grub after grub and beetle after beetle. *Tap-tap-ta-ta-ta-tap. Tap-tap-ta-ta-ta-tap!* They pecked and they pecked until Sugar Maple's itch was completely gone.

"Wonderful!" cried Sugar Maple. "I thank you all good friends."

"We thank *you* for the beetle feast," Woodpecker and his cousins replied.

Long afterward, there came a time of drought. Poor Woodpecker, half dead with thirst, came to rest on one of Sugar Maple's boughs. *"Help!"* he croaked.

"Quickly, good friend," cried Sugar Maple. "Hop to my trunk and make a hole. Make as many as you like, so that you can drink my sap when it begins to drip."

Tap-tap-tap-ta-ta-ta-tap! tapped Woodpecker. As the sweet sap dripped, he drank and drank until he was full—and found it so good that woodpeckers have been drinking it ever since.

Source: Jane Louise Curry, *Turtle Island, Tales of the Algonquian Nations.* New York: Margaret K. McElderry Books, 1999.

Paul Revere's Ride

by Henry Wadsworth Longfellow

"Paul Revere's Ride" is one of the most famous poems about our country's history. It was published by Henry Wadsworth Longfellow in 1863, in the middle of the Civil War. The poem looks back to the beginning of an earlier war—the American Revolution. It celebrates the night that the silversmith Paul Revere and two other men rode through the countryside to Concord, Massachussets, to warn the American Patriots that the British were about to attack. Thanks to the warning, the colonists were able to prepare for battle. This selection from Longfellow's even longer poem captures the danger and excitement of Revere's mission. Read the poem slowly and try to tell in your own words what is happening in each section.

Listen, my children, and you shall hear
Of the midnight ride of Paul Revere,
On the eighteenth of April, in Seventy-five;
Hardly a man is now alive
Who remembers that famous day and year.

He said to his friend, "If the British march   **He:** Paul Revere
By land or sea from the town tonight,
Hang a lantern **aloft** in the **belfry** arch   **aloft:** high up
Of the North Church tower as a signal light,—   **belfry:** a tower where
One, if by land, and two, if by sea;   bells are hung
And I on the opposite shore will be,
Ready to ride and spread the alarm
Through every **Middlesex** village and farm,   **Middlesex:** county north
For the country folk to be up and to **arm**."   of Boston
                                                                                   arm: take up weapons

48

Then he said, "Good-night!" and with **muffled** oar
Silently rowed to the Charlestown shore,
Just as the moon rose over the bay,
Where swinging wide at her **moorings** lay
The *Somerset,* British **man-of-war;**
A phantom ship, with each mast and **spar**
Across the moon like a prison bar,
And a huge black hulk, that was magnified
By its own reflection in the tide.

Meanwhile, **his friend,** through alley and street,
Wanders and watches with eager ears.
Till in the silence around him he hears
The **muster** of men at the **barrack** door,
The sound of arms, and the tramp of feet,
And the measured tread of the **grenadiers,**
Marching down to their boats on the shore.

Then he climbed the tower of the Old North Church,
By the wooden stairs, with **stealthy** tread,
To the belfry-chamber overhead,
And startled the pigeons from their perch
On the **sombre** rafters, that round him made
Masses and moving shapes of shade,—
By the trembling ladder, steep and tall,
To the highest window in the wall,
Where he paused to listen and look down
A moment on the roofs of the town,
And the moonlight flowing over all.

… A moment only he feels the spell
Of the place and the hour, and the secret dread
Of the lonely belfry and **the dead;**
For suddenly all his thoughts are bent
On a shadowy something far away,
Where the river widens to meet the bay,—
A line of black that bends and floats
On the rising tide, like a bridge of boats.

muffled: wrapped in something to soften the sound

moorings: ropes and anchors
man-of-war: armed ship
spar: pole

his friend: the one who is to send signal with lights

muster: gathering
barrack: housing for soldiers
grenadiers: soldiers

stealthy: secretive

sombre: dark and gloomy

the dead: in church cemetery

Meanwhile, impatient to mount and ride,
Booted and **spurred**, with a heavy stride
On the opposite shore walked Paul Revere.
Now he patted his horse's side,
Now gazed at the landscape far and near,
Then, **impetuous**, stamped the earth,
And turned and tightened his **saddle-girth**;
But mostly he watched with eager search
The belfry-tower of the Old North Church,
As it rose above the graves on the hill,
Lonely and **spectral** and sombre and still.
And **lo!** as he looks, on the belfry's height
A glimmer, and then a gleam of light!
He springs to the saddle, the **bridle** he turns,
But **lingers** and gazes, till full on his sight
A second lamp in the belfry burns!

A hurry of hoofs in a village street,
A shape in the moonlight, a bulk in the dark,
And beneath, from the pebbles, in passing a spark
Struck out by a **steed** flying fearless and **fleet**:
That was all! And yet, through the gloom and the light,
The fate of a nation was riding that night;
And the spark struck out by that steed in his flight,
Kindled the land into flame with its heat. . . .

It was twelve by the village clock,
When he crossed the bridge into Medford town.
He heard the crowing of the cock,
And the barking of the farmer's dog,
And felt the damp of the river fog
That rises after the sun goes down.

It was one by the village clock,
When he galloped into Lexington.
He saw the **gilded weathercock**
Swim in the moonlight as he passed,
And the meeting-house windows, blank and bare,
Gaze at him with a spectral glare,
As if they already stood **aghast**
At the bloody work they would look upon.

spurred: wearing spurs to urge horse forward

impetuous: suddenly, energetically

saddle-girth: strap used to hold saddle in place

spectral: ghostly

lo!: Look!

bridle: horse's reins

lingers: stays

steed: horse

fleet: fast

gilded weathercock: gold-coated weather vane

aghast: filled with horror

50

It was two by the village clock,
When he came to the bridge in Concord town.
He heard the **bleating of the flock**,
And the twitter of birds among the trees,
And felt the breath of the morning breeze
Blowing over the meadows brown.
And one was safe and asleep in his bed
Who at the bridge would be first to fall,
Who that day would be lying dead,
Pierced by a British **musket-ball**.

You know the rest. In the books you have read,
How the British Regulars fired and fled,—
How the farmers gave them ball for ball,
From behind each fence and farm-yard wall,
Chasing the red-coats down the lane,
Then crossing the fields to emerge again
Under the trees at the turn of the road,
And only pausing to fire and load.

So through the night rode Paul Revere;
And so through the night went his cry of alarm
To every Middlesex village and farm,—
A cry of **defiance** and not of fear,
A voice in the darkness, a knock at the door,
And a word that shall echo forevermore!
For, **borne** on the night-wind of the Past,
Through all our history, to the last,
In the hour of darkness and **peril** and need,
The people will waken and listen to hear
The hurrying hoof-beats of that steed,
And the midnight message of Paul Revere.

bleating of the flock: crying of sheep

musket-ball: bullet

defiance: bold opposition

borne: carried

peril: danger

The Old North Church in Boston, in whose tower the two famous lanterns were hung, still stands. Outside it now stands a statue of Paul Revere. Why do you think Longfellow admired Paul Revere's ride? What message do you think he might have wanted his poem to carry to the people of his own day, in the midst of the Civil War?

Source: Henry Wadsworth Longfellow, "Paul Revere's Ride," *Anthology of American Poetry*. New York: Crown Publishers, Inc., 1983.

Hard Times at Valley Forge

by Joseph Martin, 1777-1778

Supplies often ran low during the American Revolution. When General George Washington's army marched to Valley Forge, Pennsylvania, in December 1777, soldiers had little food, clothing, or medicine. One of the soldiers in Washington's army was Joseph Martin, a 17-year-old boy from Milford, Connecticut. Martin kept a diary of those hard times. How do you think people survive such hardships?

The army was now not only starved but naked. The **greatest part** were not only shirtless and barefoot, but **destitute** of all other clothing, especially blankets. I **procured** a small piece of raw cowhide and made myself a pair of moccasins, which kept my feet (while they lasted) from the frozen ground, although, as I well remember, the hard edges so **galled** my ankles, while on a march, that it was with much difficulty and pain that I could wear them afterwards; but the only **alternative** I had was to **endure** this inconvenience or to go barefoot, as hundreds of my companions had to, till they might be tracked by their blood upon the rough frozen ground. But hunger, nakedness and sore shins were not the only difficulties we had at that time to **encounter**; we had hard duty to perform and little or no strength to perform it with.

The army. . . marched for the Valley Forge in order to take up our winter **quarters**. We were now in a truly **forlorn** condition,—no clothing, no **provisions** and as disheartened as need be. . . . Our **prospect** was indeed **dreary**. In our miserable condition, to go into the wild woods and build us **habitations**. . . in such a weak, starved and naked condition, was appalling in the highest

greatest part: most
destitute of: lacking
procured: got

galled: scraped

alternative: choice
endure: put up with

encounter: deal with

quarters: housing
forlorn: sad
provisions: goods, especially food
prospect: situation
dreary: gloomy
habitations: places to live

degree. . . . However, there was no **remedy**, no alternative but this or **dispersion**. But dispersion, I believe, was not thought of, at least, I did not think of it. We had engaged in the defense of our injured country and were willing, nay, we were determined to **persevere** as long as such hardships were not altogether **intolerable**. . . .

We arrived at the Valley Forge in the evening [December 18]. It was dark; there was no water to be found and I was **perishing with** thirst. I searched for water till I was weary and came to my tent without finding any. **Fatigue** and thirst, joined with hunger, almost made me desperate. I felt at that instant as if I would have taken **victuals** or drink from the best friend I had on earth by force. I am not writing fiction, all are **sober realities**. Just after I arrived at my tent, two soldiers, whom I did not know, passed by. They had some water in their canteens which they told me they had found a good distance off, but could not direct me to the place as it was very dark. I tried to beg a **draught** of water from them but they... [refused]. At length I persuaded them to sell me a drink for three **pence**, Pennsylvania currency, which was every cent of property I could then call my own, so great was the necessity I was then reduced to.

I lay here two nights and one day and had not a **morsel** of anything to eat all the time, **save** half of a small pumpkin, which I cooked by placing it upon a rock, the skin side uppermost, and making a fire upon it. By the time it was heat[ed] through I devoured it with as keen an appetite as I should a pie made of it at some other time.

remedy: cure
dispersion: breaking up of the army

persevere: continue
intolerable: unbearable

perishing with: dying of

fatigue: tiredness

victuals: food
sober realities: hard truths

draught [draft]: drink

pence: pennies

morsel: scrap
save: except for

Nearly 3,000 soldiers died at Valley Forge during the winter of 1777–1778—roughly 30 soldiers a day. If the British had attacked they probably could have won an easy victory over the sick and starving American army. But the British never tried. In February 1778 Baron von Steuben, a German officer, came to Valley Forge and helped train and reorganize the troops. Soon American soldiers were healthy and ready for battle. Joseph Martin grew healthier, too, and served in the army until the war's final day. He then became a schoolteacher and laborer and settled in Prospect, Maine.

Source: Joseph Martin, *A Narrative of Some of the Adventures, Dangers and Sufferings of a Revolutionary Soldier.* Hallowell, Maine, 1830; reprinted Boston: Little, Brown & Company, 1962.

The Memory Coat

By Elvira Woodruff

People from countries all over the world have immigrated to the United States to find religious freedom. In this selection you will read about a Jewish family who left Russia to come to America in the early 1900s. Two young cousins comfort themselves during their journey by playing a storytelling game. Unfortunately, their fanciful stories cannot overcome their greatest fear: What will happen if the family is sent back to Russia?

It had been barely a year ago that Grisha had come to live with Rachel's family. He had been orphaned when he lost his parents in an **epidemic.** And there were still times when he would run to the alley behind the **synagogue** where he could be alone to grieve.

> **epidemic:** large outbreak of a disease
> **synagogue:** a Jewish house of worship

At these times, Rachel's mother and grandmother worried about Grisha being outdoors in the cold, with only his threadbare coat to keep him warm. But whenever they offered to make him a new one, Grisha always refused.

"I like my coat the way it is," he would tell them sharply, and he'd race out into the icy wind.

Then Rachel would throw on her own warm, woolen coat and fly out the door to comfort him.

Grisha always found great comfort in their storytelling game. And once they began, the game could last for hours.

Then one day, news spread through the marketplace that the **cossacks** were coming on powerful horses and waving sharp swords. They were looking to kill anyone who was Jewish.

> **cossack:** a member of the cavalry in the czarist Russian army

"Russia is no longer a safe place for us to live," their grandfather whispered late that night, as the frightened family gathered together.

"We must not wait for our children's blood to color the snow," Rachel's father added. "We must go to America. In America, they will be safe."

But the tales that frightened them the most were of those immigrants who had given up so much and traveled so far, only to be turned away at a place called Ellis Island, an inspection station in New York's harbor. There, immigrants were inspected to be sure they were healthy, and had enough money, and could take care of themselves.

"There will be no mistakes," Rachel's father said.

"Then we'll have to do something about Grisha's coat," Bubba decided. "Look how torn and tattered it's become. If we're to make a good impression, he will have to have a new one. Come, Grisha, let me measure your arms."

"No!" Grisha cried. He grabbed the coat and ran to the attic to hide.

"Tsk, tsk, tsk," his aunts and uncles clucked and shook their heads. "What can he see in such an old coat?"

"He sees the inside," Rachel whispered. "It's lined with the beautiful wool from his very own mother's coat. Inside, he can still feel his mama's touch."

"Ah." Their grandfather's sad sigh filled the room. Everyone lowered their eyes, ashamed at having forgotten how Grisha's dear mother had struggled to make him the little coat in the last winter of her life. Not another word was spoken about it, and Bubba took out her basket to mend the coat once more.

And so it was that this family made its way to a long line of people, to the place called Ellis Island. And so it was that Grisha's tattered coat made its way with them.

They waited in one line, then another, then another. To still their fears, Rachel and Grisha continued their game.

"Once there lived a magical bird with golden feathers," Rachel began. As she told her story, Rachel spread her arms and pretended to fly. But she suddenly lost her balance and fell against Grisha. The two tumbled down and knocked over Bubba's basket beside them. Rachel was unhurt, but Grisha scratched his eye on the basket's lid.

By the time his turn came to be examined, Grisha's injured eye looked quite red and irritated. When the doctor lifted Grisha's eyelid with a buttonhook, Grisha cried out in pain. Taking a quick look, the doctor marked a large letter "E" in chalk on the back of Grisha's coat.

Rachel felt her Bubba's hand tightening around her own as everyone began to talk at once. Something was wrong. Something was happening to Grisha. He hadn't passed the inspection. He was going to be sent back to Russia!

Suddenly, Rachel had an idea. Quickly, she pulled off Grisha's coat and turned it inside out, exposing the beautiful wool from his mother's coat.

Now the dreaded chalk mark was hidden from view, and Rachel's father was able to walk Grisha over to another line where he was examined once more. This doctor was kinder and more patient. And he understood Yiddish. He took a closer look at Grisha's eye and saw it was only a scratch. So he kept his chalk in his pocket and Grisha passed through with the rest of the family!

Bubba hugged Rachel and Grisha tight. "You were right, Grisha," Bubba said. "This coat of yours is very special. Your mama's touch will be with you for a very long time. Not only here on the outside—but here," she said, tapping Grisha's chest. "On the inside. The most important place of all."

Do you think The Memory Coat *is a good title for this book? Why?*

Source: Elvira Woodruff, *The Memory Coat*. New York: Scholastic Press, 1999.

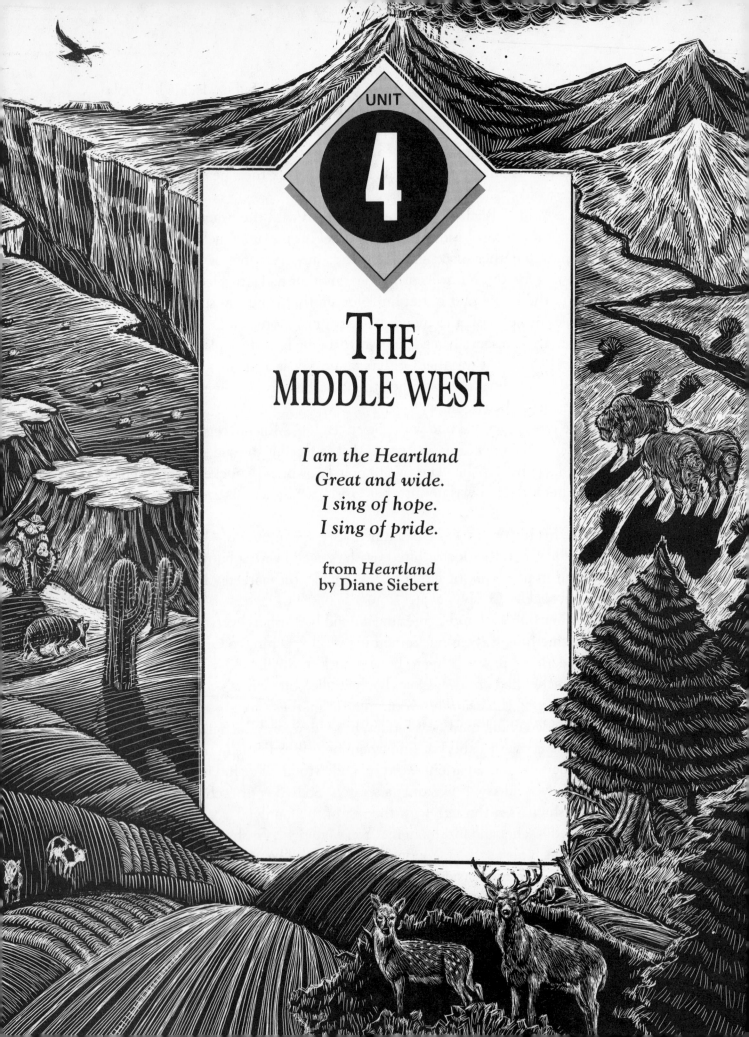

THE MIDDLE WEST

I am the Heartland
Great and wide.
I sing of hope.
I sing of pride.

from *Heartland*
by Diane Siebert

The Big Rivers

by Bruce Hiscock

Imagine waking up one morning to find the street in front of your house flooded with water. Within hours the water level has reached your front steps. You quickly pack whatever you can and leave your home. When you shut the front door, you're not sure if you will ever return. That afternoon you're helping your neighbors make sandbags to strengthen the levees along the river. This might sound like a fictional story, but it really happened to the people who lived in the Mississippi River Valley during the great flood of 1993. This is an actual account of the flood, one of the worst ever seen on the Mississippi, Missouri, and Ohio rivers. The author, Bruce Hiscock, made three trips to the rivers while working on the book from which this excerpt was taken. During the worst of the flooding, he helped fill sandbags, took photos, and drew sketches. He also interviewed many people there, including farmers, engineers, boat crews, and kids. What do you think it was like to live in the Mississippi River Valley during the great flood of 1993? How do you think the volunteers felt as they worked together making sandbags to strengthen the levees?

Spring is an uncertain time for people who live near the big rivers: the Missouri, the Mississippi, and the Ohio. These rivers cross the center of the United States, and each spring when the snow begins to melt and the rains return, the rivers start to rise. Small streams may swell quickly from the runoff, but the big rivers react in slow motion. The swirling water comes up quietly, steadily, and with enormous power. Then families watch from the riverbanks, hoping the water will not rise too fast and bring another disastrous flood.

As spring turned into summer that year, it began to rain hard in the Midwest. Rain is the lifeblood of rivers and a part of the water cycle. All rivers are created from water that evaporates, mostly from the ocean, and then falls back on the land as rain and snow. The water then flows down the rivers to the ocean, completing the cycle. When the weather is normal, the rivers can easily handle the flow, and the water cycle goes on without much notice.

But in the summer of 1993, the normal weather pattern in the Midwest changed. Humid air, full of moisture from the Gulf of Mexico, streamed north creating massive thunderstorms as it clashed with cool air from Canada. This "rain machine" stalled over Iowa, Missouri, and neighboring states, drenching some places with two to five inches of rain each day. At the same time along the Ohio River, where it is usually quite rainy, the weather was dry.

In late June, flooding started in Minnesota and Iowa sending the first crest of high water down the Misissippi. A warning call went out. **Levees** were checked. Supplies of sandbags and sand were prepared. Families who lived on low areas got ready to move.

levee: an embankment built along a river

Then, as if to tease everyone, the rain slacked off for a while, only to come back harder than ever. The lower Missouri River pushed over its banks, flooding thousands of acres of farmland with two or three feet of water.

Smaller rivers rose quickly now. The **surging** Raccoon River in Des Moines, Iowa, flooded the water purification plant despite the seventeen-foot-high levee protecting it. In Des Moines, there was water everywhere, but none of it was fit to drink.

surging: a swelling movement

The flooding was some of the worst ever seen on the Missouri and Mississippi rivers. Over one hundred thousand homes, stores, and factories were flooded, along with vast areas of farmland. People and animals were drowned. Miles of roads and railroad tracks were washed away. Bridges were closed. Plants that treat waste water became overloaded from the rain, forcing towns to let raw sewage flow into the rivers. Since many towns take their drinking water from the rivers, extra precautions were needed to make the water safe to use.

The great flood of '93 lasted longer than most floods— over a month in some places. But eventually the storms ended, and then the enormous job of cleaning up the smelly, soggy mess began. It wasn't much fun, but floods have always been a part of life along the river.

During the Great Flood of 1993, volunteers made millions of sandbags, trying to save their farms, homes, and towns. They worked in the rain and the heat; however, the flood was one of the worst ever. Flood waters covered eight million acres in nine Midwestern states and fifty people died.

Source: Bruce Hiscock, *The Big Rivers.* New York: Atheneum Books, 1997.

Bringing the Prairie Home

by Patricia MacLachlan

Where we live influences how we live. A person who grows up in the Rocky Mountains may have a different view of life than someone who grows up in a busy city. In this essay Patricia MacLachlan says she became who she is because of the prairie, or grassland, of the Middle West. What do you think she means when she says that "Earth is history"?

Place.

This is one of my favorite words and I am a writer because of it.

Place.

I remember **vividly** the place where I was born: the smell of the earth, the look of the skies when storms came through; the softness of my mother's **hollyhock** blooms that grew by the back fence.

When I was ten years old, I fell in love with place. My parents and I drove through the prairie, great stretches of land between small towns named wonderful names like Spotted Horse, Rattlesnake, Sunrise. We stopped once for drinks that we fished out of cold-water lift-top tanks, and my mother and I walked out onto the prairie. Then my mother said something that changed my life forever. She took a step, looked down at her footprint, and said, "Someone long ago may have walked here, or maybe no one ever has. Either way it's history."

vividly: clearly

hollyhock: tall plant with large, showy flowers

59

I thought of those who might have come before me and those who might come after, but mostly I was face-to-face with the important, hopeful **permanence** of place, place that I knew was there long before I walked there, and would be there long after I was gone. I realized, in that moment, that the Earth is history. The Earth is like a character who has secrets; the Earth holds important clues to who we are, who we've been; who we will be. We are connected to the land and to those secrets.

It was after this event that I bought a diary and began writing all sorts of truths about myself, as if I, too, might leave clues about myself behind. I was becoming a writer. All because of place. Now I cannot write a story unless I know the place, the **landscape** that shapes the story and the people in the story. And to remind myself of the place that changed me, I have carried a small bag of prairie dirt with me for years.

I took that bag of prairie dirt with me once to a class of fourth graders, and I found that those children are connected to place, too. Some had moved from place to place many times: One boy's house had burned in a fire recently; another was about to move to a place he had never been.

"Maybe," I said, "I should toss this out onto my New England yard. I'll probably never live on the prairie again."

"*No!*" cried a boy, horrified. "It might blow away!"

And then a girl had a suggestion.

"Maybe you should put that prairie dirt in a glass on your windowsill, so you can see it when you write. It would be like bringing the prairie home."

And that is where that little piece of my prairie is today; my place, my past, my landscape; in a glass on my windowsill. I have brought the prairie home so that I can look at it every day; write about it, write about me, and remind myself that the land is the connection that links us all.

MacLachlan brought a bag of prairie dirt to her new home to remind her of the land where she was born. If you were to save something to remind you of the place where you live, what object would you choose? Why?

Source: Patricia MacLachlan, "Bringing the Prairie Home," *The Big Book of Planet Earth.* New York: Dutton Children's Books, 1993.

Heartland

by Diane Siebert

The food grown by American farmers feeds the people of the United States and many people around the world. In her poem "Heartland," Diane Siebert celebrates the farmers of the Middle West, their fields of corn and wheat, and their herds of cattle and sheep and pigs. What makes the flat land of the Middle West good for farming? What do you think Siebert means when she writes that on the plains of the Heartland "nature reigns"?

I am the Heartland.

Hear me speak

In voices raised by those who seek

To live their lives upon the land,

To know and love and understand

The secrets of a living earth—

Its strengths, its weaknesses, its worth;

Who, Heartland born and Heartland **bred,**   **bred:** raised

Possess the will to move ahead.

I am the Heartland.

I survive

To keep America, my home, alive.

I am the Heartland.

Smell the fields,

The rich, dark earth, and all it yields;

The air before a coming storm,

A newborn calf, so damp and warm;

The dusty grain in barns that hold

The bales of hay, all green and gold.

For I have learned of drought and hail,

Of floods and frosts and crops that fail,

And of tornadoes as they move...

In frightening paths, again to prove

That in the Heartland, on these plains,

Despite Man's power, Nature **reigns**.

reigns: rules

Before me, summer stretches out

With pastures **draped** in **lush**, green grass,

And as the days of growing pass,

draped: covered
lush: thick

I feel the joy when fields of grain

Are blessed by sunlight, warmth, and rain;

And winter, white and cold, **descends**

descends: falls

With blizzards howling as they sweep

Across me, piling snowdrifts deep.

Then days grow longer, skies turn clear,

And all the gifts of spring appear—

The young are born, the **seedlings** sprout;

seedlings: young
green plants

    I am the Heartland:

        Earth and sky

And changing seasons passing by.

I feel the touch of autumn's chill,

And as its colors brightly spill

Across the land, the growing ends,

        I am the Heartland.

        In my song

Are cities beating, steady, strong,

With footsteps from a million feet

And sounds of traffic in the street;

Where giant mills and stockyards **sprawl**,

sprawl: stretch out

And neon-lighted shadows fall

From windowed walls of brick that rise

Toward the clouds, to scrape the skies;

Where highways meet and rails **converge**;

Where farm and city rhythms **merge**

To form a **vital** bond between

The concrete and the fields of green.

       I am the Heartland.

         On these plains

Rise elevators filled with grains.

They mark the towns where people walk

To see their neighbors, just to talk;

Where farmers go to get supplies

And sit a spell to **analyze**

The going price of corn and beans,

The rising cost of new machines;

Where steps are meant for shelling peas,

And kids build houses in the trees.

       I am the Heartland.

         On this soil

Live those who through the seasons **toil**:

The farmer, with his spirit strong;

The farmer, working hard and long,

A feed-and-seed-store cap in place,

Pulled down to shield a weathered face—

A face whose every crease and line

Can tell a tale, and help define

A lifetime spent beneath the sun,

A life of work that's never done.

By miles of wood and wire stretched

Around the barns and pastures where

The smell of **livestock** fills the air.

These are the farms where hogs are bred,

The farms where chicks are hatched and fed;

The farms where dairy cows are raised,

The farms where cattle herds are grazed;

converge: come together to one point

merge: blend, join

vital: very important

analyze: think about

toil: work

livestock: farm animals

The farms with horses, farms with sheep—
Upon myself, all these I keep.
A patchwork quilt laid gently down
In hues of yellow, green, and brown
As tractors, plows, and planters go
Across my fields and, row by row,
Prepare the earth and plant the seeds
That grow to meet a nation's needs.

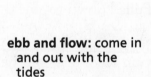

       I am the Heartland.

        I can feel
Machines of iron, tools of steel,
Creating farmlands, square by square—
A quilt of life I proudly wear:

       I am the Heartland.

        Shaped and lined
By rivers, great and small, that wind
Past farms, whose barns and silos stand
Like treasures in my fertile hand.

       I am the Heartland.

        Great and wide.

         I sing of hope.

         I sing of pride.
I am the land where wheat fields grow
In golden waves that **ebb and flow**;
Where cornfields stretched across the plains
Lie green between the country lanes.

ebb and flow: come in and out with the tides

The Middle West has some of the darkest, richest soil in the world. The region has sometimes been called the Corn Belt and sometimes the Breadbasket. Why do you think Diane Siebert calls it the Heartland?

Source: Diane Siebert, *Heartland*. New York: Thomas Y. Crowell, 1989.

A Boy Named ABE
by Susan Nanus

Abraham Lincoln, the sixteenth President of the United States, was born in a log cabin in the woods of Kentucky. When he was seven his family moved to Indiana. Always an eager student, young Abe loved to spend his time reading. Later in life he became a lawyer. He served a term in Congress and was elected President in 1860. The Civil War was fought during Lincoln's term of office, and he had the difficult job of seeing our country through the bloodiest period in its history. The play A Boy Named Abe *shows the kind of strengths the young Lincoln had as a child. Which of these qualities do you think helped him to become a leader?*

CAST OF CHARACTERS
Sally Lincoln, *Abe's older sister and story narrator*
Abe Lincoln, *now in his teens*
Tom Lincoln, *Abe's father*
Nathaniel Brown, *a wealthy neighbor*
Josiah Crawford, *a farmer*
Mrs. Crawford, *a farmer*
Dennis Hanks, *Abe's cousin*
James Taylor, *a storekeeper*

Mrs. Taylor, *a storekeeper*
Gentleman
John Dill, *a ferryman*
Martha Dill, *John's wife and partner in the ferry business*
Squire Samuel Pate, *a justice of the peace*

Time: *the 1820s*
Setting: *Pigeon Creek, Indiana*

The almost-bare stage divides into two sections: indoor scenes, stage right; outdoor scenes, stage left. Signs can be set up on chairs to indicate the different locations.

Abe is sitting cross-legged in the woods, reading.

Sally: *(enters downstage right and addresses the audience)* Our play, which is mainly about my brother, Abe, begins in the woods by our cabin.

Tom Lincoln enters.

Tom: *(calling out)* Abe! Abe Lincoln, where are you?

Sally: *(to the audience)* That's my brother Abe over there reading. He's always getting in trouble because he loves books so much.

Tom: *(finding Abe reading)* There are a hundred things to do, and I won't have you wasting time!

Nathaniel Brown, a well-dressed man, enters stage left.

Nathaniel: Tom Lincoln?

Tom: Mr. Brown, what are you doing here?

Nathaniel: Your wife said I could find you out here in the woods. *(He pulls out a paper from his coat.)* I have the deed right here.

Abe: Deed?

Tom: Mr. Brown is going to buy some land behind the cabin. Eighteen acres to be exact. Right, Mr. Brown?

Nathaniel: That's right, Tom. Now, I brought a pen and some ink, so if you'll just sign your name.... (*He pulls out a quill pen and a little bottle of ink.*)

Abe: Uh, Pa—would you like me to read the deed?

Nathaniel: There's no need for you to read it. Everything is in perfect order.

Abe: You shouldn't sign something without knowing what's in it, Pa.

Tom: Hmm. You may be right. Okay. Take a look.

Tom hands the deed to Abe, who begins to read. Tom leans to look at the deed. Nathaniel Brown sneaks away, stage left.

Abe: Just what I thought.

Tom: What?

Abe: If you sign this, Pa, he'll get the whole farm.

Tom: What! You mean he tried to cheat me? Why, you . . . (*He looks around, sees that Nathaniel is gone.*) Well, Abe, looks like for once your reading came in pretty handy.

Sally: After that, Pa doesn't bother Abe so much about his reading. A couple of years go by. Abe is the tallest, strongest boy in Pigeon Creek. Now other folks pay to have him work on their farms. This is what happens in the Crawfords' kitchen.

The Crawfords enter. Josiah has an account book and pen. Mrs. Crawford begins to make an apple pie. Abe enters stage right.

Josiah: Well, Abe, you've been both a farmhand and carpenter this week. You plowed and planted the back field, repaired the barn roof, and built a new fence. I guess I owe you a pretty penny for all that.

Abe: Yes, Sir.

Mrs. Crawford: If you'll wait a while, I'll have some fresh-baked apple pie for you.

Abe: Thanks, Mrs. Crawford, but I better get home. Only . . .

Josiah: Well, what is it, boy? Speak up.

Abe: I was wondering . . . if you don't mind . . . if I could maybe borrow one of those books? (*He points to an imaginary bookshelf.*)

Josiah: You hear that, Mrs. Crawford? Abe prefers a book to a piece of your pie!

Abe: Oh, I'm sorry, I didn't mean . . .

Mrs. Crawford: Nonsense, Abe. I know what you meant. And you just help yourself to any book on that shelf.

Abe: Thank you! (*He approaches the shelf and reads the titles.*) I think I'll take *The Life of George Washington* by Mason Weems. (*He takes the book from the shelf gently.*) I really want to study him.

Josiah: Abe, with all this studying, you'll go far. Maybe as far as Washington! (*He laughs at his joke.*)

Mrs. Crawford: Oh, Josiah! That really wasn't funny!

The Crawfords exit stage right, as Abe starts reading.

Sally: (*setting up The Lincolns' Cabin sign*) That night, Abe stays up half the night, reading his new book.

As Sally speaks, Abe closes the book and puts it in a crack in the wall between two imaginary logs. Then Abe gets into bed and falls asleep.

Sally: Abe sleeps in the loft. There's a big storm. Rain drips through the cracks and . . . the book is ruined! Our cousin Dennis finds Abe the next day.

Dennis enters stage right and walks to Abe.

Dennis: What's the matter? You sick or something?

Abe: Look what happened to Mr. Crawford's book! I don't believe it! It's all wet and wrinkled from the rain.

Dennis: Oh, boy! You're in for it now. What will you say? The cabin burned down? A robber stole it?

Abe: I'd sure like to have an excuse, but I don't. I guess I'll just have to tell Mr. Crawford the truth.

Dennis: Old Honest Abe, huh, boy?

Abe: I guess so, Dennis.

Sally: So Abe goes and tells Mr. Crawford just what happened. *(As she speaks, Josiah Crawford enters.)*

Josiah: That book cost a lot of money, Abe.

Abe: I know, Sir.

Josiah: And money doesn't grow on trees.

Abe: I know, Sir.

Josiah: Lending you the book was generous on my part.

Abe: Indeed it was, Sir.

Josiah: It was your responsibility to take good care of it.

Abe: *(looking down)* Yes, Sir.

Josiah: Well, it was an accident. But you can work off the cost. Three days in the fields should do it.

Abe: *(gratefully)* Yes, Sir. And . . . here's the book. *(He holds it out.)* You can still read the pages inside.

Josiah: You want it? You can have it. As long as you don't read it on the job. Now, get to work!

Abe: Yes, Mr. Crawford. And thank you. Thank you so much!

Josiah and the others clear the chairs, leaving the table as a store counter. Josiah exits stage right as the Taylors enter and stand on one side of the counter, Abe on the other.

Sally: In 1825, Abe is 16. He helps the Taylors run their store. The store is at Posey's Landing on the bank of Anderson's Creek, close to the Ohio River. Steamboats go up and down the Ohio, and there's a ferry that takes folks from here to the other side of the river, where the boats dock. The Taylors are about to leave on a trip.

James: Now remember, Abe. The beans are over there and the flour is in the back.

Mrs. Taylor: We don't give credit, remember that.

Abe: Yes, Ma'am.

James: *(pointing)* Nails and other hardware over here.

Mrs. Taylor: No money, no merchandise.

Abe: Yes, Mrs. Taylor.

James: *(nodding toward an imaginary shelf)* Cloth and dress patterns on the shelf.

Abe: You know, it's getting late.

James: He's right! Come on, Mrs. Taylor, we've a coach to catch, and the driver doesn't plan to wait for us. (*James takes her arm, and they exit.*)

Abe: (*goes to the door and peers in both directions*) No customers in sight, so . . . (*He pulls a book from his pocket and begins to read.*)

A gentleman rushes into the store.

Gentleman: (*with agitation*) Quick! That rowboat outside. Whose is it?

Abe: Well, it's mine, but—

Gentleman: I'll give you two dollars to row me out to the steamboat right now.

Abe: Well . . . okay. Let's go.

The two rush stage left to an imaginary rowboat. Abe pantomimes rowing it.

Sally: But what Abe thinks is a good deed almost gets him into trouble.

The Dills enter stage left and stand on the riverbank, watching as Abe approaches.

Sally: The Dills own the ferry that takes passengers from the shore across the river to where the boats dock.

John: (*showing disbelief*) Do you see what I see, Martha?

Martha: How dare he! Who is he?

John: It's Abe Lincoln. The Pigeon Creek boy who works for the Taylors. He could steal our business, Martha.

Midstream, the gentleman climbs out of the rowboat and onto the steamboat and exits stage left. Abe starts rowing back to the store.

John: Hey, you! Abe Lincoln!

Martha: Come over here a minute, will you?

Abe: What for?

Abe reverses direction and rows toward the Dills.

John: Don't you know you can't ferry people across the river without a
   license? You've broken the law!

Martha: We have a license, and you don't!

John: You're coming with us, young man!

Martha: If the Justice of the Peace finds you guilty, you'll be thrown
   in jail!

*Martha takes one of Abe's arms; John takes the other. They half-lead,
half-pull him stage right as Squire Samuel Pate, carrying his gavel, enters
the courtroom from stage right.*

Sally: And that is how Abe comes to meet Squire Samuel Pate, Justice
   of the Peace, who is holding forth right now.

Squire Pate: Order! Order in the court. State your case.

John: Your Honor, Martha and I have a license to ferry passengers
   across the river. And we caught this boy red-handed rowing a man
   to the steamboat.

Squire Pate: (*to Abe*) What do you say to that, young man?

Abe: What he says is true. But their license is to carry folks across the
   river. I only went to the middle. So I don't think I really broke
   the law.

Squire Pate: (*pulling out a thick book and leafing through it*) The law is
   plain. You two have the right to set a person across, but there's no
   law against rowing passengers to midstream.

John: What! But that's not fair!

Squire Pate: (*banging his gavel*) Quiet! Case closed.

John and Martha storm out stage left.

Squire Pate: You've got a good head on your shoulders, young man. What's your name?

Abe: Abraham Lincoln, Sir. I'm interested in the law.

Squire Pate: Then you should read this book. Knowing the law of the land never hurts.

Abe takes the book reverently.

Squire Pate: Would you like to come to my court and listen in sometime?

Abe: You would let me do that, Your Honor?

Squire Pate: Yes I would. I believe you want to learn. And I'd not be surprised if you want to do something big with what you learn. Am I right?

Abe: I hope I can, Sir. I will surely try.

Squire Pate: Young man, I expect great things of you.

Sally: And that's how Abe took his first step toward being a lawyer and after that a congressman and after that . . . well, you already know. Abe was always determined to learn and to do something good with what he learned. Thank you, Squire Pate, for helping Abe take that first important step.

There are many stories told about Abraham Lincoln's youth. Some might be true, some might be made up, but all are entertaining. The writer of this play chose a few stories that she had read about Abraham Lincoln and dramatized them—or made them into scenes in a play. If you wanted to do the same, how could you find additional stories about Lincoln's life to dramatize? What kind of story do you think would make a good scene?

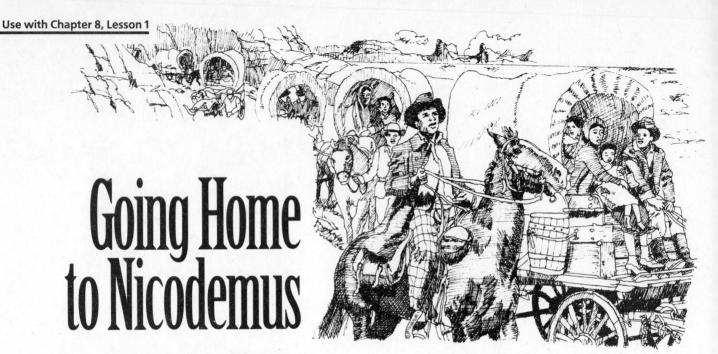

Going Home to Nicodemus

by Daniel Chu and Bill Shaw

Going Home to Nicodemus tells the true story of the town built by African Americans who traveled west to the frontier territory of Kansas after the Civil War. These pioneers, nearly all of them freed slaves, were part of a huge migration, as settlers headed west in search of the free land promised by the Homestead Act of 1862. This selection introduces Nicodemus through the experience of Willianna Hickman and her family, who were among the first settlers in Nicodemus. What did Mrs. Hickman think when she first saw the town? Why do you think she and the others decided to stay?

The year was 1878, and Willianna Hickman found herself in a place she had never been before. Kansas was its name, and it was, Willianna had been told, the "Promised Land."

Willianna Hickman was thirty-one years old and a woman of color. This was one of the terms commonly used in the nineteenth century to describe an African American. Willianna and her husband, the Reverend Daniel Hickman, had traveled to Kansas from Georgetown, in north central Kentucky where the Reverend Hickman had been the minister of the Mount Olive Baptist Church.

All but the youngest in Daniel's Kentucky **congregation** had been born in slavery. But now, thirteen years after the end of the American Civil War, they were free men and women. No longer could they be bought and sold as property to be kept or **disposed of** at the whim of masters.

congregation: church group

disposed of: gotten rid of

74

For all of that, however, America's leaders had not given enough thought as to what was to become of the four million freed slaves in the South. The freed men and women owned neither land nor homes and had little, if any, money. Most could not read or write. During slavery, they had **toiled** on southern plantations as field hands or household servants. They knew little else.

toiled: worked

Now they were at liberty to leave the plantations and go wherever they wished. But where would that be? How were they to feed and house themselves? Where would they find work? How could people who had so little survive?

For the members of Reverend Hickman's church group, an answer came during the winter of 1877–1878. It came in the person of a white visitor named W. R. Hill.

W. R. Hill was a land **promoter** from Kansas, far away to the west. Hill told the Georgetown church members that there was government land available for **homesteading** on the western frontier. There was lots of it, and it was practically free for the asking. To claim a quarter section of land—160 acres—a homesteader had little more to do than show up.

promoter: person who organizes and furthers a business plan

homesteading: claiming and settling on land granted by United States government for farming

Think of it! How could someone who had nothing, and no way of getting anything, turn down an offer like that?

The idea of homesteading became more attractive as Hill talked on. He and his partners had put together a special package for blacks only: a new town on the prairie run by blacks **exclusively** for blacks. Even as he spoke, W. R. Hill confided, hundreds of black settlers already were moving to this new community, a town that bore an **intriguing** name: Nicodemus.

exclusively: only

intriguing: curiosity-arousing

To the Georgetown, Kentucky, church audience on that wintry night, W. R. Hill's words were like an answered prayer. Here was a chance, the first for any of them, to own a piece of land, to be independent and self-supporting, to make their own way in life. It was a chance to leave behind the racial **hostility** and discrimination they had always known.

hostility: show of hatred

Out on the open plains of the Kansas frontier, W.R. Hill said, blacks and whites would live as equals.

With the coming of spring, about two hundred members of the Reverend Hickman's church packed up their few belongings and joined the great western **migration**. From the hills of Kentucky, they went off in two groups for Kansas and a new life.

migration: movement

The migrants from Kentucky reached Ellis in western Kansas by rail in just a few days. But an outbreak of measles among the children brought sudden tragedy. Some of them died, but Daniel and Willianna Hickman and their six children were among the luckier ones. They survived the outbreak. After a two-week delay in Ellis, the Hickmans and the other families hired horses and wagons for the final leg of their journey.

What a journey it was!

Guided by compass, they traveled two more days across roadless plains marked here and there by a few trees, deer trails, and buffalo wallows, or watering holes. At night the men built roaring campfires and fired their guns in the air to keep wild animals away. The women unpacked bedding and cooked a meal while the children slept or played games within the shadow of the fire's glow.

Worn from travel, Willianna Hickman was almost totally **spent** by the time her group arrived at its destination. She felt even worse when she got her first look at it.

spent: exhausted

Nicodemus was not the Promised Land she had expected, not what she had hoped for. To Willianna's **dismay**, there lay before her an entire community of people living in holes in the ground. The people were **burrowed** into the earth like the prairie dogs Willianna had seen on the trek from Ellis.

dismay: frightened amazement

burrowed: dug

More than a half century later, when she was ninety, Willianna Hickman still **vividly** remembered her shock and astonishment on that spring day in 1878:

vividly: clearly

When we got in sight of Nicodemus, the men shouted, "There is Nicodemus." Being very sick, I hailed this news with gladness. I looked with all the eyes I had. "Where is Nicodemus? I don't see it." My husband pointed out various smokes coming out of the ground and said, "That is Nicodemus." The families [there] lived in dugouts. ... The scenery was not at all inviting, and I began to cry.

—Topeka [Kansas] *Daily Capital*, 1937

...Despite her crushing disappointment, Willianna Hickman, her family, and their fellow pioneers did not turn back. The rough conditions of life on the western frontier, in circumstances so lacking in comforts, stunned even those who had experienced the cruelties of slavery. The new hardships they faced were many, more than enough to discourage all but the bravest and strongest.

Most of the pioneers from Kentucky stayed. They **coped** and endured. They held to their hopes and dreams and kept their faith. And because they and their children did what they did, Nicodemus has survived as the oldest—and now the only remaining—all-black frontier town on the Great Plains.

coped: struggled successfully

The holes in the ground that greeted Willianna Hickman are long gone now, but Nicodemus is still there.

What do you think attracted settlers to Nicodemus? How do you think those who stayed were able to turn Nicodemus into a thriving frontier town?

Source: Daniel Chu and Associates, *Going Home to Nicodemus*. Morristown, NJ: Silver Burdett Press, 1994.

The Buffalo Go

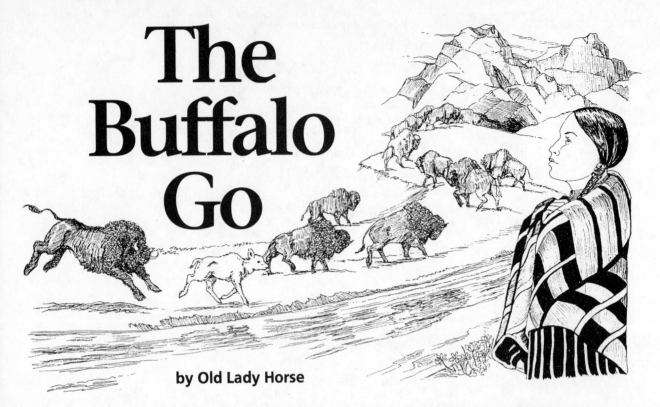

by Old Lady Horse

For hundreds of years giant herds of buffalo roamed the Great Plains of the Middle West. Many Indian groups, such as the Kiowa, depended on the buffalo for food, clothing, and shelter. In the late 1800s hunters began killing all of the buffalo. In the legend below, a Kiowa woman named Old Lady Horse describes what happened to the buffalo and her people.

Everything the Kiowas had came from the buffalo. Their tepees were made of buffalo hides, so were their clothes and moccasins. They ate buffalo meat. Their containers were made of hide, or of bladders or stomachs. The buffalo were the life of the Kiowas.

Most of all, the buffalo was part of the Kiowa religion. A white buffalo calf must be sacrificed in the Sun Dance. The priests used part of the buffalo to make their prayers when they healed people or when they sang to the powers above.

So, when the white men wanted to build railroads, or when they wanted to farm or raise cattle, the buffalo still protected the Kiowas. They tore up the railroad tracks and the gardens. They chased the cattle off the ranges. The buffalo loved their people as much as the Kiowas loved them.

There was war between the buffalo and the white men. The white men built forts in the Kiowa country, and the . . . buffalo soldiers shot the buffalo as fast as they could, but the buffalo

78

kept coming on, coming on, even into the post cemetery at Fort Sill. Soldiers were not enough to hold them back.

Then the white men hired hunters to do nothing but kill the buffalo. Up and down the plains those men ranged, shooting sometimes as many as a hundred buffalo a day. Behind them came the skinners with their wagons. They piled the hides and bones into the wagons until they were full, and then took their loads to the new railroad stations that were being built, to be shipped east to the market. Sometimes there would be a pile of bones as high as a man, stretching a mile along the railroad track.

The buffalo saw that their day was over. They could protect their people no longer. Sadly, the last **remnant** of the great herd gathered in council, and decided what they would do.

remnant: remaining part

The Kiowas were camped on the north side of Mount Scott, those of them who were still free to camp. One young woman got up very early in the morning. The dawn mist was still rising from Medicine Creek, and as she looked across the water, peering through the haze, she saw the last buffalo herd appear like a spirit dream.

Straight to Mount Scott the leader of the herd walked. Behind him came the cows and their calves, and the few young males who have survived. As the woman watched, the face of the mountain opened.

Inside Mount Scott the world was green and fresh, as it had been when she was a small girl. The rivers ran clear, not red. The wild plums were in blossom, chasing the red buds up the inside slopes. Into this world of beauty the buffalo walked, never to be seen again.

The next selection is a poem about the loss of the buffalo. As you read it, think about what these two pieces have in common.

Source: Alice Marriot and Carol K. Rachlin, *American Indian Mythology*. New York: Thomas Y. Crowell Company, 1968.

79

Hitting the Road
Automobile Advertisements,
1902 and 1924

The first automobiles were invented in the late 1800s. These early cars took a long time to build and cost anywhere from $1,000 to $3,000. Most Americans at that time earned less than $1,000 a year. As a result, only wealthy people could afford to buy cars. Many people, however, benefited from the jobs generated by the new automobile industry. You have read how thousands moved to Detroit and other Great Lake cities to find work with the car manufacturers.

When Henry Ford set up an assembly line in his factory in 1913, production time and costs were greatly reduced. Look at the advertisements below. The one on the left is from 1902, and the one on the right is from 1924. How do the cars compare in price and looks?

The
Haynes-Apperson

is the only automobile that has been consistently developed through 10 years of successful experience on American Roads.

THE same development that has given foreign cars their reputation has given the Haynes-Apperson its proved reliability, but because of the more severe conditions in this country there is no car of equal horse power that will last as long, handle as easily, and ride as smoothly on American Highways as this American product.

> Runabout, 7 Horse Power, 2 Passengers, $1200
> Phaeton, 12 Horse Power, 2 Passengers, $1500
> Surrey, 12 Horse Power, 4 Passengers, $1800

Ask our Customers
Get our Booklet

Delivery in ten days on immediate orders

Haynes-Apperson Co., Kokomo, Ind.

Ford
Touring Car
$295

F. O. B. DETROIT
Starter and Demountable Rims $85 Extra

OF all the times of the year when you need a Ford car, that time is NOW!

Wherever you live—in town or country—owning a Ford car helps you to get the most out of life.

Every day without a Ford means lost hours of healthy motoring pleasure.

The Ford gives you unlimited chance to get away into new surroundings every day—a picnic supper or a cool spin in the evening to enjoy the countryside or a visit with friends.

These advantages make for greater enjoyment of life—bring you rest and relaxation at a cost so low that it will surprise you.

By stimulating good health and efficiency, owning a Ford increases your earning power.

Buy your Ford now or start weekly payments on it.

Henry Ford's automobiles changed life in the United States forever. At such low prices, many people could afford to buy cars. Soon new highways—dotted with gasoline stations, motels, and restaurants—crisscrossed the nation. People used cars to get to work, to go shopping, and to visit friends. With automobiles now available for transportation, many Americans began leaving cities and moving to nearby areas. Suburbs soon began to grow. How do automobiles affect life today?

Working the Land

by Pierce Walker

In 1972 the writer Studs Terkel interviewed Pierce Walker, an Indiana farmer. When he was a boy, Pierce Walker lived on a farm of 80 acres. As an adult, he had a farm of 250 acres, and he worked an additional 250 acres for other people. How did Pierce Walker feel about the technology—that is, the new machines— that he used to farm his land?

Farming, it's such a gamble. The weather and the prices, and everything that goes with it. You don't have too many good days. It scares you when you see how many working days you actually have. You have so many days to get the crop planted and the same in the fall to harvest it. They have this all figured down to the weather. It tenses you up. Whether we needed rain or we didn't need rain, it affects you in different ways. I have seen a time when you're glad to hear the thunder and lightning. Then again, I've wished I didn't hear it. (Laughs). . .

Weather will make ya or break ya. The crops have to have enough moisture. If they don't have enough, they hurt. If you have too much, it hurts. You take it like you git. There's nothing you can do about it. You just don't think too much about it. My wife says it doesn't bother me too much. Of course, you still worry. . . .

I don't believe farmers have as much **ulcers** as business people 'cause their life isn't quite as fast. But I'll say there will be more as times goes on. 'Cause farming is changing more. It's more a business now. It's getting to be a big business. It's not the labor any more, it's the management end of it.

Your day doesn't end. A farmer can't do like, say, a doctor— go out of town for the weekend. He has to stay with it. That's just one of the things you have to learn to live with. I'd say a majority of the time a farmer, when he comes in at night and

ulcers: stomach problems

81

goes to bed, he's tired enough he's not gonna have trouble sleepin'. Of course, he'll get wore down. . . .

My father-in-law helps me an awful lot in the spring and a little in the fall. He drives the tractor for me. My daughter, she drives a tractor when school is out. When I was home there on the farm, there were five children, three boys, and we were on an eighty-acre farm. It took all of us, my father and three boys. You can see the difference machinery plays in it.

The number of farmers is getting less every day and just seems like it's getting worse every year. The younger ones aren't taking over. The majority of the people **originated** from the farm years ago. But it's been so long ago that the young ones now don't realize anything about the farm. What goes with it or anything like that. The **gamble** that the farmer takes.

originated: started

gamble: risk

The city people, when they go to the grocery store and the price of meat is raised, they jump up and down. They don't realize what all is behind that. They're thinking of their own self. They don't want to put up that extra money—which I don't blame them either. The same way when I go to buy a piece of equipment. I go jump up and down. . . .

When you get a good crop, that's more or less your reward. If you weren't proud of your work, you wouldn't have a place on the farm. 'Cause you don't work by the hour. And you put in a lot of hours, I tell you. You wouldn't stay out here 'til dark and after if you were punchin' a clock. If you didn't like your work and have pride in it, you wouldn't do that.

You're driving a tractor all day long, you don't talk to anyone. You think over a lot of things in your mind, good and bad. You're thinking of a new piece of equipment or renting more land or buying or how you're going to get through the day. I can spend all day in the field by myself and I've never been lonesome. Sometimes I think it's nice to get out by yourself. . . .

This interview comes from a book by Studs Terkel. Terkel wanted to know how all different kinds of Americans felt about their jobs, so he traveled around America asking them and tape-recording their answers. If you could interview a farmer in the Middle West today, what questions would you ask?

Source: Studs Terkel, *Working*. New York: Random House, Inc., 1972.

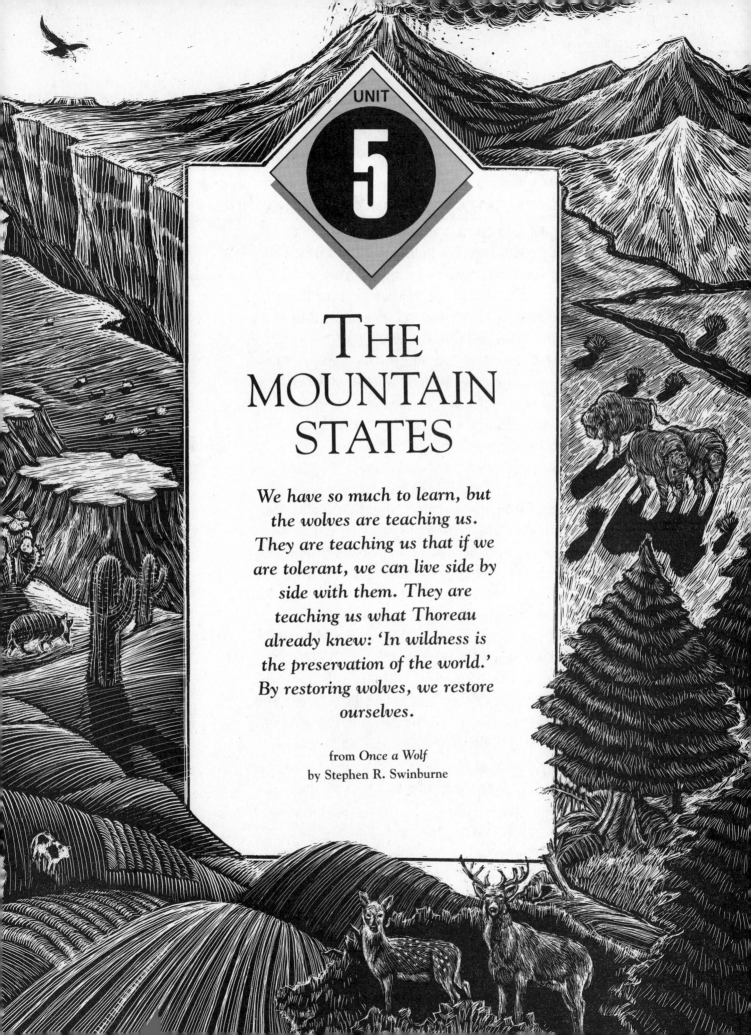

THE MOUNTAIN STATES

We have so much to learn, but the wolves are teaching us. They are teaching us that if we are tolerant, we can live side by side with them. They are teaching us what Thoreau already knew: 'In wildness is the preservation of the world.' By restoring wolves, we restore ourselves.

from *Once a Wolf*
by Stephen R. Swinburne

Legends of Landforms
"Mateo Teepee"
retold by Carole G. Vogel

This is a legend told by the Cheyenne, a Native American group that migrated to the Great Plains in the 18th century. What does this legend explain?

A band of people once camped in the rugged, pine-studded hills of what is now Wyoming. No one knew what hostile tribes or **ferocious** beasts might be lurking in the wilderness. So the fathers and the mothers warned their children to stay close to camp until scouts searched the countryside and determined the dangers.

ferocious: fierce

However, as the men hunted and the women prepared the noon meal, seven young maidens wandered away. The girls meant to obey, but the day was so pleasant and the countryside so beautiful they forgot the warnings. The maidens **pranced** and played in the sunlight.

pranced: to move in a proud way

Seemingly out of nowhere a pack of ferocious grizzly bears came upon them. Terrified the maidens raced back toward the camp. Growling and **gnashing** their teeth, the bears gave chase and easily closed the gap. Just as the grizzlies were about to pounce, the girls leaped onto a rock.

gnashing: to strike or grind

Immediately the rock began to grow upward, lifting the girls away from the bears. Higher and higher it stretched as the angry bears jumped and clawed at its sides. But the sides were too smooth and too steep. Try as they might, the bears could not reach the top.

The bears finally gave up and headed down the column. They were so tired, they slipped, and crashed to the ground.

Peering down from the top of the column, the girls saw the grizzlies fall. Anxiously they scrutinized the battered bodies, looking for signs of movement. When they saw none, the maidens gathered together the flowers they had picked, and braided them into a long rope. Then one by one they scrambled down the rope until all seven girls reached the ground.

The bodies of the bears have long vanished. Their claw marks, however, can still be observed on the side of Mateo Teepee.

What do you find interesting about this legend?

Source: Carole G. Vogel, *Legends of Landforms.* Connecticut: Millbrook Press, 1999.

84

Once a Wolf
by Stephen R. Swinburne

Through deliberate killing and the altering of the wolf's environment we were very close to losing one of our greatest predators and destroying a valuable part of our ecosystem. The excerpt below discusses the troubled relationship between man and wolf and the movement that has restored the wolf to the wild. As you read, think about the importance of predators in nature. Why is it important to be respectful of the balance of nature?

To carry out the mandate of the Endangered Species Act, the federal government formed the Northern Rocky Mountain Wolf Recovery Team. This team tackled the issue of when and how to bring wolves back into the western United States. In 1982, they released their plan, which called for wolves to be returned to two places in the West, including Yellowstone, by 1987.

While biologists and **bureaucrats** were thinking through their plans to bring the wolves back, the western ranching community was fighting hard to keep wolves out. "The time of the wolf is over," one sheep rancher said. "The wolf is like the buffalo and the dinosaur; his time has come and gone."

bureaucrats: an official who follows a rigid routine

Despite public support for returning wolves to Yellowstone, the powerful livestock industry and **influential** western politicians **hampered** plans for the program. To most ranchers, reintroducing wolves was like inviting a murderer home for dinner. And many ranchers swore they'd deal with wolves in their own way – "Shoot, shovel, and shut up!" Wolf recovery symbolized unwanted change and was seen as a tool for the government to gain more control over property rights.

influential: to have an effect on
hampered: interfered

In 1981 a young wildlife biologist named Renee Askins stepped into the **fray**. She had studied wolves in Michigan and Indiana. Her passion for them matched the intensity of the anti-wolf ranching crowd. Armed with a scientist's knowledge of the facts and a gift for public speaking and media relations, Askins mounted a dynamic campaign on behalf of the wolves. In 1986 she founded the Wolf Fund to help return wolves to Yellowstone.

fray: dispute

Askins took her message out on the road and into the heart of the **foe**. "When I talk about the wolf issue," said Askins, "I talk about the importance of wildness in our lives. It's wildness that heals us. We need contact with it, regardless of whether we live in the city or in the Alaskan wilderness—

foe: an enemy

the way wolves move, the way they play, their unpredictability, their living on the edge of their **endurance** and surviving out there."

endurance: survival

Ranchers felt that wolf recovery was being pushed down their throats by rich city people and easterners living far from any ranch. "They have the luxury of not worrying about livestock losses," the rancher would claim.

"All the science, the studies, the experts, and the facts show that wolves kill far less than one percent of the livestock available to them," Askins often emphasized. "More cows and sheep die each year because of storms and dogs or because they've rolled over onto their backs and can't get up. The real issue is one of making room, and there is still a little room in the West—room for hunters, for environmentalists, for ranchers, and for wolves."

While Askins's Wolf Fund educated the public nationwide about the Yellowstone wolf issue, groups such as Defenders of Wildlife also played a key role. In 1985 Defenders sponsored an exhibit called "Wolves and Humans" at Yellowstone. More than 200,000 park visitors saw the exhibit. Defenders also established, a few years later, a simple and **innovative** plan: the wolf compensation fund. The idea was to pay ranchers for any livestock killed by wolves. This went a long way to weaken the argument that livestock producers would bear the financial burden of the wolf reintroduction. Defenders' first payment was made in the summer of 1987, when a pack of Canadian wolves moved into Montana and attacked and killed ten sheep and five cows. A month later Defenders sent checks totaling $3,000 to the ranchers who lost livestock.

innovative: new

In 1986 David Mech, [a wolf researcher] came out strongly in favor of restoring wolves. "The only thing missing in Yellowstone is the wolf, " said Mech. "And the park can't really be wild without it. It's not complete or natural wilderness to have the species of prey that are there and not have the main predator they evolved with."

On January 12, 1995 at 8:35 A.M., a female wolf along with seven others of her kind were reintroduced to Yellowstone National Park. It's too early to tell how wolves will change Yellowstone, but many scavengers like grizzly bears, magpies, eagles, foxes and wolverines are benefiting from the leftover wolf kills.

Source: Stephen R. Swinburne, *Once a Wolf*. Boston: Houghton Mifflin Company, 1999.

Off the Map, The Journals of Lewis and Clark

edited by Peter and Connie Roop

In 1803 at the request of President Thomas Jefferson, Meriwether Lewis and William Clark led an expedition to explore the land that the United States had just purchased from France, known as the Louisiana Territory. Their job included exploring the Missouri River and finding a safe passage west to the Pacific Ocean. President Jefferson asked them to write a description of everything they saw on their expedition. Why do you suppose President Jefferson wanted this? Below is a journal entry from their expedition.

August 17, 1805. Saw several Indians on horseback coming. The interpreter and squaw danced for the joyful sight, and she made signs that they were her nation. The meeting of these people was really affecting, particularly between Sacagawea and an Indian woman who had been taken prisoner with her, and who had afterward escaped and rejoined her nation. The great chief Cameahwai proved to be Sacagawea's brother and is a man of influence, sense, easy, and reserved manners. Everything astonished these people—the appearance of the men, their arms, the canoes, the clothing, my black servant, and the **sagacity** of Captain Lewis's dog.

sagacity: cleverness

August 26, 1805. We arrived at the extreme source of the Missouri. Here we halted for a few minutes. The men drank of the water and consoled themselves with the idea of having at length arrived at this long-wished-for point.

September 2, 1805. Set out early. Proceeded on through thickets, over rocky hillsides where our horses were in **perpetual** danger of slipping to their certain destruction. One horse crippled, two gave out.

perpetual: everlasting

November 7, 1805. Great joy in camp. We are in view of the ocean, this great Pacific Ocean, which we have been so long anxious to see, and the roaring made by the waves breaking on the rocky shores may be heard distinctly.

The Lewis and Clark expedition left St. Louis, Missouri, in May 1803, and reached the Pacific Ocean in November 1805. Lewis and Clark mapped and explored over 3,000 miles of land, making it easier for new settlers to find their way west.

Source: Peter and Connie Roop, *Off the Map: The Journals of Lewis and Clark.* New York: Walker and Company, 1993.

DOTY'S WASHER

Advertising Poster from the 1800s

In the late 1800s, technology was advancing in leaps and bounds in the United States. Between 1860 and 1900, the first automobiles, telephones, telegraphs, electric lamps, and radios were produced. Cameras and sewing machines, invented in the early 1800s, became popular. People were urged to buy all kinds of wonderful new machines. The advertising poster below shows a washing machine of the 1800s—"Doty's Clothes Washer" with the new "Universal Clothes Wringer." In what ways do you think a new machine like the "Doty's Clothes Washer" changed the lives of women?

THE PAST.   THE PRESENT.

HOUSEKEEPERS, TAKE YOUR CHOICE.

DOTY'S CLOTHES WASHER, lately much improved, and the new UNIVERSAL CLOTHES WRINGER, with Rowell's Expansion Gear, and the patent "Stop," save their cost twice a year by saving clothes, besides shortening the time and lessening the labor of washing nearly one-half.

A FAIR OFFER.—Send the retail price:—WASHER, $14; EXTRA COG-WHEEL WRINGER, $9—and we will forward to places where no one is selling, either or both, free of charges. If, after a trial of one month, you are not entirely satisfied, we will REFUND THE MONEY on the return of the machines, FREIGHT FREE.   **R. C. BROWNING, General Agent,**

Large Discount to the Trade everywhere. **32 Cortlandt St., New York.**

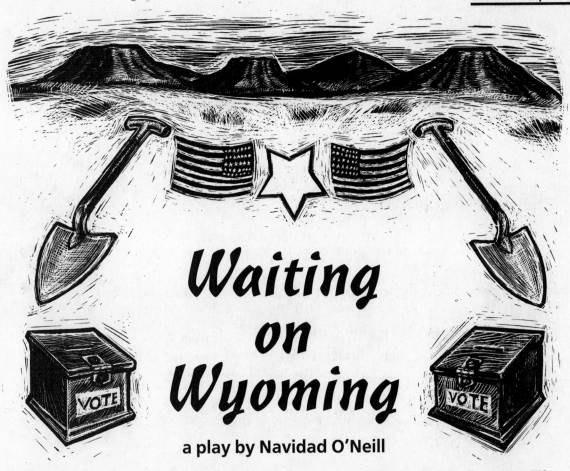

Waiting on Wyoming

a play by Navidad O'Neill

You have read that until 1919 women could not vote in national elections. The struggle for voting rights—or suffrage— for women gained support in the West, where men and women worked side by side and many people were open to new ideas. The territory of Wyoming passed a law in 1869 allowing women to vote in its elections, making it the first place in the country where women could vote. This play takes place on the day the first ballots were cast by Wyoming women. Why was this such an exciting moment? How did people in other parts of the country feel about this event?

CAST OF CHARACTERS

Esther Morris

Mr. Morris, her husband

Son 1
Son 2 } *the Morrises' sons*
Son 3

Reporter

Grandma Swain

Poll Attendant

Miner

Chorus of newspaper editors

Editor 1

Time: *Early morning, December, 10, 1869.*
Setting: *The Morrises' general store in the territory of Wyoming.*

One area should be identified as a polling place, and another as a kitchen. The chorus, seen throughout the play, should be located in a newspaper office, "back East."

At the store, Son 1 and Esther tug at a CLOSED sign. The other members of the Morris family look on.

Son 1: But Ma, today is December Tenth!

Mr. Morris: I agree, Esther. No one will mind if you close the shop.

Son 2: You've been working so hard for this day to happen. You've been talking to all the legislators, talking to the neighbors...

Esther: But people depend on this store. I am going to open it for them, like I do every day, even though today *is* the first day the women of Wyoming will vote in an election.

Mr. Morris: The first day women *anywhere* in our country will vote.

Esther: That's true but you know what I say: Neither rain, nor snow, nor fleet of rattlesnakes can close my shop.

She turns the sign from CLOSED to OPEN. Reporter comes rushing in.

Reporter: The mail in?

Mr. Morris: Came early this morning.

Mr. Morris pulls out a large sack of letters.

Esther: I've already taken my letters.

She shows a large pile. Mr. Morris empties his sack, begins sorting the letters.

Reporter: Wow! There's enough of them, isn't there? Why, here's a letter from my editor.

Son 3: Mama, what's an editor?

Esther: An editor runs a newspaper. Decides what stories should be written.

Mr. Morris: And whether the stories are important enough to go on the front page.

Reporter: Listen to this:

Editor 1 steps out of chorus. As Reporter reads we hear Editor speak.
Lines could also be divided up among chorus members.

Editor 1: Dear Dan, my man, in Wyoming.
　　We want to hear all about what happens when women vote
　　for the first time. Everyone back East expects that there will be
　　many problems. Wyoming is so new and seems pretty rough to us
　　back home in the East. Is it true there aren't even cobblestones on
　　the street yet? Is it true that there are miners who actually sleep on
　　the side of mountains to protect their claims? How will such men
　　act when they have to share their voting rights? Let us know
　　everything. We also want to know who will be the first woman
　　to vote.

Grandma Swain enters the shop as the Reporter continues to read.

Editor 1: Get her name. What she says. Especially any trouble that
　　happens. It's up to you, Dan, my man. We will hold our breath
　　until we hear from you. We plan on sharing your stories with other
　　newspapers up and down the coast. Send us a telegraph as soon as
　　you can.
Reporter: You bet I will.

Chorus: We're waiting. We're waiting.
　　Waiting on Wyoming news!
　　We're waiting. Anticipating.
　　Send us hints, please! Send us clues!

Grandma Swain: Lovely morning isn't it?

Esther: Good morning to you, Grandma Swain.

Grandma Swain: Yes, it is a good morning and I plan to enjoy every minute of it. Esther, I'll take one of those tins of blueberry preserves on that top shelf of yours.

Esther: Sure, Grandma Swain. Anything else?

Grandma Swain: Any cherry syrup?

Esther: One last bottle.

Grandma Swain: I'll take that too.

She pays for the purchases.

Esther: Why the special ingredients, Grandma Swain? This isn't your usual grocery order.

Grandma Swain: I'm fixing myself a red, white and blue breakfast today.

Grandma Swain exits. Walks over to her kitchen area.

Son 2: Good thing we had the store open, Ma. Grandma Swain would have been disappointed if we had been closed.

Son 3: What are all those other letters?

Reporter: All seem to be predictions.

Son 1: What's a prediction?

Reporter: When a person announces beforehand what is going to happen later.

Son 3: But no one knows the future.

Mr. Morris: A lot of people think they do, like that editor who thinks that just because the mountains are rugged, people living in Wyoming must all be rough too.

Chorus: We're waiting. We're waiting.
Waiting on Wyoming news!
We're waiting. We're waiting.
For that place to blow a fuse!

Grandma Swain in her kitchen.

Grandma Swain: Two cups of flour...one cup of blueberries. Mix well.

Reporter: You see, son, there are suffragists and anti-suffragists.

Son 2: I know Mama's a suffragist because she wants women to vote.

Son 1: So does an anti-suffragist not want Mama to vote?

Mr. Morris: An anti-suffragist doesn't want *any* women to vote.
Including herself, if she is a her.

Reporter: And anti-suffragists want me to include their predictions in
my story.

Reporter rips open a letter.

Reporter: They say: If women have the right to vote, they will leave
their kitchens and hang out on the street smoking cigars all day.

Son 2: You'd never do that, would you, Ma?

Esther: You know I hate cigar smoke.

Grandma Swain is now eating pancakes.

Grandma Swain: Hmmmm. Hmm. Blueberry pancakes with cherry
syrup and whipped cream. For a star-spangled morning.

Reporter rips open another letter.

Reporter: They say: Women don't know enough about current events
to vote wisely.

Son 3: But Ma keeps up with what's happening, just like Pa.

Reporter rips open another letter.

Reporter: Here's another. They say: If women try to vote on December 10th, there will be fights. Some angry men will try to stop the women at the poll booths.

Sons 1, 2, 3: Ma, maybe you shouldn't vote!

Esther: Well, children, I say, the country is like a general store. If there's an OPEN sign on the door, then anyone can come in and do business. You don't hang a CLOSED sign up for some customers and an OPEN sign for others. But it's taking a while for our country to open the election place to all. It used to be closed to men who didn't own property. And until recently it was closed to African American men. And it's still closed to all women.

Grandma Swain has finished eating. She stands up.

Grandma Swain: I've waited 75 years for this day.

Chorus: We're waiting. We're waiting.
Waiting on Wyoming news!
We're waiting. Anticipating.
What should we, back East, conclude?

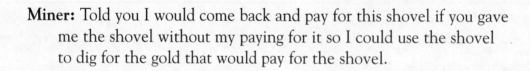

Enter a miner with a shovel.

Miner: Told you I would come back and pay for this shovel if you gave me the shovel without my paying for it so I could use the shovel to dig for the gold that would pay for the shovel.

Esther: I knew you would. You're an honest man.

Miner: Okay if I pay in gold nuggets?

Esther: Sure.

Miner pays in gold nuggets.

Miner: And I thank you for trusting me. Trust is what makes a person feel part of the community. Now I'm off to find some more gold.

Esther: Well, good luck to you. And your shovel.

Miner: And I want you to know, Esther Morris, I never voted in any election before. But today I'm planning on voting, too. I figure if you think it's so important—then, well, maybe it is.

Miner exits.

Mr. Morris: Boys, 'you think you can handle things at the store while your mother and I go to cast our votes?

Sons: Sure.

Son 2: We love to be in charge!

Reporter: Do you mind if I go with you?

Esther: The more the merrier.

They all move from the store onto the street area.

Mr. Morris: Look, there's Grandma Swain.

Grandma Swain at the polling place. She folds a piece of paper and hands it to poll attendant.

Grandma Swain: Here's my ballot, sir.

Poll Attendant: Why thank you kindly, Grandma Swain. You can put it right in the box.

Grandma Swain: *(She does.)* I hope I've served as an example. Voting is the peaceful way to make changes. *(She walks up to the group. To Reporter:)* Write that in your story.

Reporter: I will.

They all shake hands.
They freeze in this celebratory position, except Reporter who speaks to the
audience as he writes with his pencil on a pad.

Reporter: The first woman to vote in the country was an elderly
Quaker woman, known to all as Grandma Swain.

Grandma Swain unfreezes and continues the story.

Grandma Swain: She began an election process that was very peaceful
throughout the territory of Wyoming—as quiet as the folding of a
paper ballot.

Poll Attendant: Twenty-one years later, when Wyoming was to become
a state, the United States Congress asked that Wyoming repeal
the right to vote for women, since the rest of the country did not
allow it.

Mr. Morris: Wyoming refused. It said it would rather wait another
100 years to become a state than become a state denying women
the right to vote.

Chorus: No more waiting! Anticipating!
The answer has come in:
Women in Wyoming win!

Esther: I guess you could say that on that day in Wyoming the polling
places were finally "open." (*She holds up the sign.*) But now our play
is "closed." (*She turns sign over to CLOSED.*)

THE END

Esther Morris of Wyoming was later elected as the first woman judge in the
United States. These important events gave Wyoming the nickname "Equality
State." What do you think it was about life in the West that made people eager
to accept equality for women?

THE WEST

I am the mountain,
Tall and grand.
And like a sentinel I stand.
Surrounding me, my sisters rise
With watchful peaks that pierce the skies;
From north to south we form a chain
Dividing desert, field, and plain.

from "Sierra"
by Diane Siebert

SIERRA

by Diane Siebert

In her poem "Sierra," Diane Siebert traces the history of the Sierra Nevada mountains. She begins with their birth millions of years ago and then describes how they changed over the years to become what they are today: a beautiful site with a great variety of plant and animal life. What are some of the plants and animals that live in the Sierra Nevada mountains today?

I am the mountain,
Tall and grand.
And like a **sentinel** I stand.   **sentinel:** guard
Surrounding me, my sisters rise
With watchful peaks that **pierce** the skies;   **pierce:** cut
From north to south we form a chain
Dividing desert, field, and plain.
I am the mountain.
Come and know
Of how, ten millions years ago,
Great forces, moving plates of earth,
Brought, to an ancient land, rebirth;
Of how this planet's **faulted crust**   **faulted:** cracked or
Was shifted, lifted, tilted, thrust   broken, resulting in
Toward the sky in waves of change   earthquakes
To form a newborn mountain range.   **crust:** Earth's
I am the mountain,   outermost layer
Young, yet old.

98

I've stood, and watching time unfold,
Have known the age of ice and snow
And felt the **glaciers** come and go.
They moved with every melt and freeze;
They shattered boulders, leveled trees,
And carved, upon my granite rocks,
The terraced walls of **slabs** and blocks
That trace each path, each downward course,
Where through the years, with crushing force,
The glaciers sculpted deep **ravines**
And polished rocks to glossy sheens.
At last this era, long and cold,
Began to lose its **frigid** hold
When, matched against a warming sun,
Its final glacier, ton by ton,
Retreated, melting, making way
For what I have become today:
A place of strength and **lofty** height;
Of shadows shot with shafts of light;
Where meadows nestle in between
The arms of forests, cool and green;
Where, out of **clefted** granite walls,
Spill silver, snow-fed waterfalls.
Here stand the pines, so straight and tall,
Whose needles, dry and dying, fall
Upon my sides to slowly form
A natural blanket, soft and warm;
Their graceful, swaying branches sing
In gentle breezes, whispering
To **junipers**, all **gnarled** and low,
That here, in stubborn splendor, grow.
And on my western slope I hold
My great **sequoias**, tall and old;
They've watched three thousand years go by,
And, in their endless **quest** for sky,
This grove of giants slowly grew
With songs of green on silent blue.
          I am the mountain.
             In each breath
I feel the pull of life and death
As untamed birds and beasts obey
The laws of **predator** and **prey**.

glaciers: huge sheets of ice

slabs: big, flat pieces of rock

ravines: valleys

frigid: icy

lofty: very high

clefted: creased

junipers: evergreen shrubs or trees
gnarled: knotted

sequoias: tallest trees in the world

quest: search

predator: an animal that hunts other animals
prey: animals hunted by predators

On me, the hunted ones reside,
Sustained by foods my plants provide:
I keep the **pikas**, small and shy,
That spread their gathered grass to dry.
I shelter rodents. In my trees
Live pinecone-loving **chickarees**,
While tunnels, **crevices**, and holes
Hold **marmots**, ground squirrels,
   chipmunks, **voles**.
I cradle herds of graceful deer
That drink from waters cold and clear;
I know each **buck** with antlers spread
Above his proud, uplifted head.
I know each doe, each spotted fawn,
In sunshine seen, in shadows, gone.
I know these creatures, every one.
They, to survive, must hide or run;
As food for those that stalk and chase,
Within life's chain, they have a place.
Then, too, the predators are mine,
Each woven into earth's design.
I feel them as they wake and rise;
I see the hunger in their eyes.
These are the coyotes, swift and lean;
The bobcats, shadowy, unseen;
The **martens** in their tree-branch trails;
The masked raccoons with long, ringed tails;
The mountain lions and big black bears
That live within my rocky **lairs**;
The owls that prowl the skies at night;
The hawks and eagles, free in flight.
I know them all. I understand.
They keep the balance on the land.
They take the old, the sick, the weak;
And as they move, their actions speak
In tones untouched by right or wrong:
     We hunt to live.
     We, too, belong.
     I am the mountain.
     From the sea
Come constant winds to conquer me—
Pacific winds that touch my face

pikas: small rodents similar to rabbits

chickarees: red squirrels

crevices: narrow openings

marmots: mountain mice

voles: a kind of rodent

buck: male deer

martens: animals like weasels

lairs: dens

And bring the storms whose clouds embrace
My rugged shoulders, strong and wide;
And in their path, I cannot hide.
And though I have the strength of youth,
I sense each change and know the truth:
By wind and weather, day by day,
I will, in time, be worn away;
For mountains live, and mountains die.
As ages pass, so, too, will I.
But while my cloak of life exists,
I'll **cherish** winds and storms and mists,
For in them, precious gifts are found
As currents carry scent and sound;
As every gust and playful breeze
Helps **sow** the seeds of parent trees;
As silver drops and soft white flakes
Fill laughing streams and alpine lakes;
As lightning fires, hot and bright,
Thin undergrowth, allowing light
To reach the fresh, cleared soil below
So roots can spread and trees can grow.
  I am the mountain,
   Tall and grand,
  And like a sentinel I stand.
Yet I, in nature's wonders **draped**,
Now see this mantle being shaped
By something new—a force so real
That every part of me can feel
Its actions changing nature's plan.
Its numbers grow. Its name is MAN.
And what my course of life will be
Depends on how man cares for me.
  I am the mountain,
   Tall and grand.
  And like a sentinel I stand.

cherish: love and
 treasure

sow: spread, scatter

draped: dressed

*Diane Siebert says that "MAN" is a new force whose actions change nature's
plans. What does she mean by this? She says that the life of the Sierra Nevada
mountains depends on how man cares for them. How do you think that people
can take care of mountains?*

Source: Diane Siebert, *Sierra*. New York: HarperCollins, 1991.

The Year of Miss Agnes
by Kirkpatrick Hill

The Year of Miss Agnes tells the story of the close relationship that develops between a teacher from England and her Athabascan students on the Koyukak River in Alaska during 1948. Told from the perspective of "Fred" a young Athabascan girl, it is a story about Alaska and the wonderful teacher who introduces her class to the world. Why is school so attractive to the narrator? Why do you think Miss Agnes is so important to the children and to the village?

Miss Agnes used a big map to teach us geography. She pointed out the continents with a yardstick, and then she showed us how to find Alaska every time.

We had to look for the old man's beard and the fat nose. The beard was all islands. The Aleutian Islands. I never knew about those.

Then she took out a folded-up map, a map of just Alaska. It was as big as two desks, so we pushed Little Pete's and Roger's desks together, and there we were.

There was the Koyukuk River, our river, and the Yukon, down below us, and all the villages, even Dolbi, our old village that no one lived in anymore. And there was Fairbanks and Anchorage. All the little creeks were there, and the long lakes and **sloughs.**

sloughs: swamps

Little Pete and Roger got just excited, showing us where their trapline was, and where they set the blackfish trap, and where their dad shot the bear. It was so interesting, somehow, seeing it there on paper. I never saw the big boys so excited about anything in school.

I asked Miss Agnes where Juneau was, and she showed me, way down at the bottom, in the part she said was called the panhandle because that part looked like a long handle and the rest of Alaska like the pan. I ran my finger from where we were on the Koyukuk River to Juneau and thought of Daddy making that long trip. It was a long way away to go to die.

Miss Agnes said she was going to teach us every one of the countries on the big map, so we'd know everything about the world. There were places where it was hot all the time and where they had never seen snow. There were places where it was cold in the winter and hot in the summer.

I could hardly wait.

After Miss Agnes folded up the big Alaska map, she gave us all a paper with arithmetic on it. She'd made one for each of us, but they were all different. Charlie-Boy's and Selina's just had numbers on them, and places to draw things. To see if they could count, like.

I was ten, so my paper had some hard adding and some take-aways. Marie's and Little Pete's and Roger's had lots more on it than mine did.

I always hated this arithmetic, and I always just wrote any old numbers down before, so I wouldn't have to think about it. And if the teachers wanted to make me do it right, I would cry and carry on. Then they would leave me alone about it.

Even if writing was fun when Miss Agnes showed us how, there was no way she could make this arithmetic fun.

After she walked around to see how many of us could do the figuring on our papers, she told us the story of Sam Dubin. That's the old man who had the mother named Frederika. Sam Dubin came from far away, too, a place above the boot. Yugoslavia or something. And then he made a store here long ago, up around Allakaket.

He made a lot of money because there were a lot of mining camps around here in the old days. And those miners would buy anything. But that old Dubin couldn't read, and he couldn't do arithmetic, only a little. After a while people began to cheat him.

And he lost all his money. He had to go back to where he came from, broke. All that money he got cheated out of because he couldn't do his arithmetic.

Miss Agnes was going to teach us so no one could cheat us. Like if we went to a trader in Fairbanks and sold our furs, when they added it up, we'd know if they **shorted** us. Or if we went to a store and gave them money, we'd know if they gave us back the wrong change. Or charged us too much. It could happen if you're not smart.

shorted: given less

So right there I made up my mind I was going to get good at this number stuff.

The Alaskan students' education complimented their environment and way of life so that they were better prepared to live in the world. How might their education be different if they lived in a city or suburb?

Source: Kirkpatrick Hill, *The Year of Miss Agnes.* New York: McElderry Books, 2000.

Kaiulani, The People's Princess, Hawaii, 1889

by Ellen Emerson White

The following is a fictionalized journal based on the real life of Hawaii's last princess, Victoria Kaiulani Cleghorn. The journal is written between 1889-1893 as Kaiulani struggles to be a better princess. The excerpt below focuses on Kaiulani's trip to Washington D.C. to speak to President Grover Cleveland about American businessmen attempting to overthrow the monarchy. Mr. Davies was Kaiulani's guardian when she traveled oversees. As you read, would you have wanted to be in her position? Why or why not?

February 18, 1893

Today after consulting again with Mr. Davies, I issued an official statement of intent to all of the London newspapers, but I hope it will be read by Americans, too.

My statement said: *Four years ago, at the request of Mr. Thurston, then a Hawaiian cabinet minister, I was sent away to England to be educated privately and fitted to the position which by the Constitution of Hawaii I was to inherit. For all these years I have patiently and in exile* **striven** *to fit myself for my return this year to my native country.*

striven: made a serious effort

I am now told that Mr. Thurston is in Washington asking you to take away my flag and my throne. No one tells me this even officially. Have I done anything wrong, that this wrong should be done to me and my people? I am coming to Washington to plead for my throne, my nation and my flag. Will not the great American people hear me?

I can only hope that the American people will be willing to <u>listen</u>.

President Cleveland agreed with Kaiulani, but the provisional government that overthrew the monarchy refused to give up their power and declared martial law. Kaiulani's pleas for her country were ignored, and when the new president, William McKinley, took office he, along with Senate approval, annexed the country of Hawaii to the United States. The next year, in 1899, Kaiulani died. She was twenty-four years-old.

Source: Ellen Emerson White, *Kaiulani, The People's Princess.* New York: Scholastic, Inc., 2001

BY THE GREAT HORN SPOON!

by Sid Fleischman

Excitement ran high in the gold fields of California in 1849. People could have no money one day and be worth $1 million the next day if gold was discovered on their claim! But it didn't always work out that way. Sid Fleischman's novel By the Great Horn Spoon! *takes place during the California Gold Rush. It is a work of historical fiction. The characters are made up, but the historical details are accurate. In this section 12-year-old Jack Flagg and Praiseworthy, the family butler, have just arrived in California. Their goal is to return to Boston with enough money to save the family home. What do they discover about life in the mining camps?*

There was road dust in Jack's eyebrows, in his ears and down his neck. Now that they had arrived he had gold fever so bad that he didn't see how he could wait another five minutes to get his shovel in the ground. . . .

It was exactly one hour and five minutes before Jack saw the **diggings.** First Praiseworthy registered at the hotel. They washed . . . "Can we go now?" said Jack, fidgeting. He had polished his **horn spoon** so much he could see his nose in it.

diggings: where the Forty-Niners panned for gold

horn spoon: a spoon made from a deer's antlers

105

"Go where?"

"The diggings."

"Oh, the diggings will still be there after lunch, Master Jack."

Praiseworthy's patience was a marvel—and an **exasperation**. They had come more than 15,000 miles and now they had to stop to eat. Jack didn't care if they passed up eating for a week. A month, even . . . .

"You and the boy want bread with your **grub**?" asked the waiter. He was a big fellow in floppy boots.

"Why not?" answered Praiseworthy.

"It's a dollar a slice."

The butler slowly arched an eyebrow.

"Two dollars with butter on it."

Praiseworthy peered at Jack, and then smiled. "Hang the cost, sir. We're celebrating our arrival. Bread and butter, if you please!"

The bear steak was greasy and stringy, but something to write home about. Jack forced it down. After they left the restaurant Praiseworthy bought a pair of buckskin pouches at the **general merchandise** store. . . . Jack liked the new leather smell of the pouch. He tucked it under his belt, next to the horn spoon, and was beginning to feel like a miner. Then, with tin **washbasins** under their arms and the pick and shovel across their shoulders, they set out for the diggings.

The day was hot and sweaty. When they reached running water they saw miners crouched everywhere along the banks. They were washing gold out of the dirt in everything from wooden bowls to frying pans.

"Anybody digging here?" asked Praiseworthy when they came to a bare spot.

"Shore is," came the answer. "That's Buffalo John's claim."

The butler and the boy moved on upstream . . . .

On and on they went, looking for a place to dig. They passed miners in blue shirts and red shirts and checked shirts and some in no shirts at all. Picks assaulted the earth and shovels flew. Weathered tents were staked to the hillsides and the smell of boiling coffee drifted through the air. After they had walked a mile and a half Jack began to think they would never find a patch of ground that wasn't spoken for.

Suddenly a pistol shot cracked the mountain air. Praiseworthy's washbasin rang like a bell and leaped from his arm and went clattering away.

exasperation: annoyance

grub: food

general merchandise: all kinds of things for sale

washbasin: washpan, a big bowl that could be used for washing your hands, your clothes, your plates—or panning for gold

"You there!" a voice from behind bellowed.

Praiseworthy turned. His eyes narrowed slowly. "Are you talking to me, sir?"

"Talkin' and shootin'. What you doin' with my washpan under your arm?"

Jack stared at the man. He had a thick, tangled beard and his ears were bent over under the weight of his slouch hat.

"Needless to say, you're mistaken," Praiseworthy answered. "Until this moment I've had the good fortune never to set eyes on you or your washpan, sir."

"We don't take kindly to thievery in these parts," growled the miner, stepping forward. "A man steals around here, we lop off his ears. That's miner's law."

"Do you have any laws against shooting at strangers?"

"Nope."

Jack couldn't imagine Praiseworthy with his ears lopped off. He took a grip on the handle of the shovel as the miner came closer. His heart beat a little faster and he waited for a signal from Praiseworthy.

The miner belted his pistol and picked up the washpan. He **crimped** an eye and looked it over.

crimped: squinted

"It's mine, all right."

"You're either near-sighted or a scoundrel," said Praiseworthy.

Jack was ready to fight, if not for their lives—at least for Praiseworthy's ears. Just then, a flash of tin in the sunlight, from a pile of wet rocks, caught Jack's eye. He dropped the shovel and went for it.

"Is this your pan?" Jack said.

The miner's bushy eyebrows shot up like birds taking wing. "It is at that, ain't it?" Then he laughed as if the joke were on him. "I'd forget my boots if I didn't have 'em on."

Praiseworthy peered at the man. Apparently, shooting at strangers by mistake didn't amount to anything in the diggings. The miner hardly gave it another thought.

Forty-Niners didn't usually include children and family servants. But in some ways Praiseworthy and Jack were typical Forty-Niners. They came to California to get rich quick and leave. And just like the other Forty-Niners, Jack and Praiseworthy realized it was not going to be nearly as easy as they had hoped.

Source: Sid Fleischman, *By the Great Horn Spoon!* Boston: Little, Brown and Company, 1963.

107

INDEX BY *Category*

INDEX BY *Title*

INDEX BY *Subject*

(continued from copyright page)

Excerpt from WALK ACROSS AMERICA by Peter Jenkins. Text © 1979 by Peter Jenkins. William Morrow & Company, Inc.

WHEN I WAS YOUNG IN THE MOUNTAINS by Cynthia Rylant. © 1982 by Cynthia Rylant. Penguin USA Inc.

Excerpt from ROSA PARKS: MY STORY by Rosa Parks. © 1992 by Rosa Parks. Penguin USA Inc.

"I, Too" from COLLECTED POEMS by Langston Hughes. © 1994 by the estate of Langston Hughes, reprinted by permission of Alfred A. Knopf, Inc.

Excerpt from WORKING by Studs Terkel. ©1972, 1974 by Studs Terkel. Pantheon Books, a division of Random House, Inc.

"Roll On, Columbia" words by Woody Guthrie. © 1936 (renewed 1964), 1950 (renewed 1985) and 1963. Ludlow Music, Inc. New York, NY.

Excerpt from THE GREAT HORN SPOON! By Sid Fleischman. © 1963 by Albert S. Fleischman. Little, Brown and Company.

"Bringing the Prairie Home" by Patricia MacLachlan from THE BIG BOOK FOR OUR PLANET. © 1993 by Patricia MacLachlan. Dutton's Childrens Books, a division of Penguin Books USA Inc. NY.

"John Greenhow's Store: Williamsburg, Virginia" from WILLIAMSBURG CRADLE OF THE REVOLUTION by Ron and Nancy Goor. © 1994 by Ron and Nancy Goor. Atheneum Books for Children, New York.

"Fall" from DOGS AND DRAGONS/ TREES AND DREAMS by Karla Kuskin. Harper & Row Publishers, Inc. New York.

"Blow, Ye Winds, In the Morning" from SEA TO SHINING SEA.

Traditional, arranged by Jerome Epstein. © 1993 Amy L. Cohn, Scholastic Inc., New York.

"Paul Revere's Ride" by Henry Wadsworth Longfellow from ANTHOLOGY OF AMERICAN POETRY. © 1983 Crown Publishers, Inc., Avenel Books.

From GOING HOME TO NICODEMUS by Daniel Chu and Bill Shaw. © 1994 Dan Chu and Associates. Julian Messner, a division of Silver Burdett Press, NJ.

"A Geyser of Oil!" from SPINDLETOP by James A. Clark and Michel T. Halbouty. © 1952 by James A. Clark and Michel T. Halbouty. © 1952 James A. Clark and Michel T. Halbouty. Random House, New York.

From SPANISH PIONEERS OF THE SOUTHWEST by Joan Anderson. © 1989 by Joan Anderson. E.P. Dutton, a division of NAL Penguin Inc., New York.

"Grand Canyon East: From the Air" from REMEMBERING AND OTHER POEMS by Myra Cohn Livingston. © 1989 by Myra Cohn Livingston. Margaret K. McElderry Books, New York.

Excerpt from THE MEMORY COAT by Elvira Woodruff. © 1999 by Elvira Woodruff. Scholastic Press, Inc., New York.

Excerpt from THE YEAR OF MISS AGNES by Kirkpatrick Hill. © 2000 by Kirkpatrick Hill. Margaret K. McElderry Books, New York.

Excerpt from OFF THE MAP: THE JOURNALS OF LEWIS AND CLARK. © 1993 by Peter and Connie Roop. Walker and Company, New York.

Excerpt from THE BIG RIVERS by Bruce Hiscock. © 1997 by Bruce Hiscock. Atheneum Books for Young Readers, New York.

Excerpt from EVERGLADES, BUFFALO TIGER AND THE RIVER OF GRASS by Peter Lourie. © 1994 by Peter Lourie. Published by Boyds Mills Press, Inc., Honesdale, PA.

Excerpt from ONCE A WOLF by Stephen R. Swinburne. © 1999 by Stephen R. Swinburne. Published by Houghton Mifflin Company, Boston.

Excerpt from SONGS FROM THE LOOM by Monty Roessel. © 1995 by Lerner Publications Company, Minneapolis, MN.

Excerpt from KAIULANI, THE PEOPLE'S PRINCESS by Ellen Emerson White. © 2001 by Ellen Emerson White. Published by Scholastic, Inc., New York.

"Woodpecker and Sugar Maple" from TURTLE ISLAND, TALES OF THE ALGONQUIN NATION retold by Jane Louise Curry. © 2000 by Jane Louise Curry. Published by Atheneum Books, New York.

"Mateo Teepee" from LEGENDS OF LANDFORMS by Carole G. Vogel. © 1999 by Carole G. Vogel. Published by The Millbrook Press, Connecticut.

Credits
Photography: 23: t. l. Marmel Studios/The Stock Market. 48:t.r. Courtesy Penguin USA. 49: b Courtesy NAACP Public Relations. 50: t. UPI/Bettman.

Illustration: Anthony Arcado 105–107; Alex Bloch 81; John Bowdren 44; Michael Bryant 35; George Guzzi 74; James Grashow 27; Janet Hamlin 2–5, 6–7, 89; Fiona King 2; Doug Knutson 52; Anni Matsick 56; Jim McConnell 65, 70; Marty Norman 48, 49; Donna Perone 27–29; Joel Rogers 18; Dennis Schofield 23, 26; Andrea Tachiera 136; Stefano Vitale 14–17

Activities

Teachers share a common goal—to help their students become successful learners who can understand, remember, and apply important knowledge and skills. This important goal is best supported when students are offered a variety of ways in which to learn.

The Social Studies Anthology offers you the rich and varied tools that you need to help your students learn. It includes such diverse sources as diaries, poems, songs, stories, legends, and posters—all of which draw students into the sights and sounds of the places and times they are studying.

You may invite students to explore the Anthology selections in many unique ways— rewriting documents in another genre, dramatizing the selection, creating posters or collages, or writing original poems, stories, and songs. We have provided an activity for teaching each selection in the Anthology. But these activities, of course, are only suggestions. You should feel free to teach the selection in any way that you feel is best suited for your own classroom.

A WALK ACROSS AMERICA

by Peter Jenkins

Pages 2–5

Use with Introduction, pp. 6–7

Objectives

- ❑ *Identify the major landforms that are described in* A Walk Across America.
- ❑ *Recognize the enormous challenge that Peter Jenkin's walk across the country represented.*
- ❑ *Trace Peter Jenkins's route across the United States on a map.*

Background Information

After students have read the selection by Peter Jenkins, remind them that the selection they have read described just one part of Jenkins's walk across the United States. Tell students that Jenkins's walk took him through the following states and cities in this order: New York; Pennsylvania; Washington, D.C.; Virginia; North Carolina; Tennessee; Georgia; Alabama (through Montgomery and then Mobile); Louisiana (through New Orleans); Texas (through Dallas up near the northwest corner of the state); New Mexico; Colorado; Utah (through Salt Lake City); Idaho (through Boise); and Oregon.

Tracing a Route

Direct students' attention to the map of United States: Physical in *Our Country's Regions* pages R20–21. As you read out the names of the states and cities Jenkins passed through, have students trace Jenkins's route on their maps. Ask volunteers to name the different types of landforms found on Jenkins's route. (mountains, hills, plateaus, plains) Ask students which of these landforms were probably the most difficult for him to cross. (Mountains probably presented him with the most difficulty; other types of landforms may have been just as difficult in bad weather conditions.) Ask students why much of Jenkins's route passed through the southern half of the United States. (Jenkins probably chose to take the southern route because weather conditions would be less harsh during the winter.)

ROLL ON, COLUMBIA

by Woody Guthrie

Pages 6–7

Use with Introduction, pp. 10–11

Objectives

- ❑ *Recognize how Woody Guthrie's song conveys the beauty and importance of the Columbia River.*
- ❑ *Identify the route of the Columbia River.*

Tracing a Route

After students have read the lyrics to the song, discuss with them why Woody Guthrie wrote a song about the Columbia River and electric power. Point out to students that the hydroelectric power from the Columbia River brought electricity to millions of people.

Have students trace the route of the Columbia River on a map of North America. Ask questions such as: *The Columbia River forms part of the border of which two states?* (Oregon and Washington) *Through what mountain ranges does it flow?* (Coast Ranges, Cascade Range) *In what other country does the Columbia River flow?* (Canada)

I HEAR AMERICA SINGING
by Walt Whitman
Page 8

I, TOO
by Langston Hughes
Page 9

Use with Introduction

Objectives

❏ *Identify how Walt Whitman uses poetry to describe his view of America.*

❏ *Identify how Langston Hughes uses poetry to describe his hopes for African Americans.*

❏ *Write a poem linking both poems to America today.*

Linking to Today

After students have read each poem, volunteers might want to read the poems aloud to the class. Discuss with students the people and workers referred to in Whitman's poem. (mechanics, carpenter, mason, boatman, and so on) Ask students to identify the line in Hughes's poem that shows it was written in response to Whitman's. ("I, too, sing America.") Ask students why they think Hughes felt the need to write a response. (because Whitman had written about ordinary people, but not people who were sent to the kitchen to eat)

Have students write a poem about America today. Encourage them to write about what they hear America singing. Students might enjoy illustrating their poems. After students have completed their poems, ask volunteers to read them to the rest of the class.

SYMBOLS OF THE NATION
Pages 10–11

Use with Introduction, p. 38

Objectives

❏ *Explain how and why symbols are used to express ideas.*

❏ *Identify important symbols of the United States.*

❏ *Create symbols to represent your school or classroom.*

Creating Symbols

Have students read the selection and examine the symbols. Then ask them why people use symbols. (as a sign to represent something, to communicate without language) Ask volunteers to describe other national symbols not mentioned in the selection. (Possible examples include Uncle Sam, the Lincoln Memorial, and the White House.)

Ask students to consider how they might use a symbol to represent their school or classroom. Have them work individually or in groups to design a symbol. Ask volunteers to write a brief description that explains their symbol. Then have them share their designs with the rest of the class. Display the symbols on the bulletin board.

GRAND CANYON EAST: FROM THE AIR

by Myra Cohn Livingston
Page 13

Use with Chapter 1, Lesson 1

Objectives

❑ *Identify the perspective the poet uses to describe the Grand Canyon.*

❑ *Identify the perspective the poet uses to compare the Grand Canyon with other objects.*

❑ *Write a new version of the poem from a different perspective.*

Exploring Perspectives

After students have read the poem, ask volunteers to identify the vantage point from which the Grand Canyon is described. (from high above) Next ask students to discuss what the poet compares the Grand Canyon to. (old apartment buildings) Ask students: *What do you think of this comparison?* (Responses will vary.)

Have students write their own versions of the poem from different perspectives of viewing the Grand Canyon. Suggestions might include: from the ground, from the inside, from the point of view of a rock or river, compared to another natural phenomenon, or compared to an object in the students' own geographical region. Display the poems, perhaps illustrated, in a canyonlike formation on the bulletin board. Encourage students to read their poems aloud or, if possible, record them for a class tape of student readings.

KATE HEADS WEST

by Pat Brisson
Pages 14–17

Use with Chapter 1, Lesson 2

Objectives

❑ *Identify some of the geographical attractions found in the Southwest as described in the selection.*

❑ *Draw postcards illustrating attractions of the Southwest.*

Drawing Your Own Postcards

After students have read the selection, discuss each postcard with them. Ask students to imagine what picture might be shown on the first postcard. (a rodeo in Forth Worth) Suggest that students skim the message on the first postcard to find clues about the picture. Then ask students: *What pictures might be on the other postcards?* (the desert, the Rio Grande or Juarez, Gila Cliff Dwellings National Monument, the petrified Forest, the Grand Canyon)

Divide the class into six groups. Have each group draw one postcard. Suggest that students reread Kate's message for possible images to use in their illustrations. After students have completed their postcards, display them on a bulletin board titled "Postcards from the Southwest."

A GEYSER OF OIL!

by James A. Clark and Michel T. Halbouty
Pages 18–20

Use with Chapter 1, Lesson 3

Objectives

❑ *Identify what a geyser is and what it does.*

❑ *Describe how drillers struck oil in Beaumont, Texas, in 1901.*

❑ *Conduct a "press conference" with the workers and townspeople who were involved in the oil strike.*

Conduct a Press Conference

After students have read the selection, write the word *geyser* on the chalkboard and guide students in making associations with other words and ideas. (Students may suggest other kinds of geysers, or other oil well images.) Next have students take turns summarizing the steps in drilling for oil. (These can be listed on the chalkboard.) Have students describe the emotional reactions of Al and Curt Hamill, Peck Byrd, Louie Mayer, Charley Ingals, Patillo Higgins, and Captain Anthony Lucas to the discovery of oil. Discuss how the town of Beaumont changed after the oil strike. (Many became rich; the oil industry boomed.)

Have students write notes on one side of a 5 × 8 card about the people involved in the discovery of "black gold" gushing from Spindletop. On the other side of the note card, students can write notes and draw diagrams of the oil drilling process. Have students prepare questions for a press conference in which people connected with the Beaumont oil discovery are interviewed by student reporters covering the story. Drawings, replicas of "black gold," and diagrams of drilling can decorate the press conference room.

SONGS FROM THE LOOM

by Monty Roessel
Pages 21–22

Use with Chapter 2, Lesson 1

Objectives

❑ *Recognize the importance of weaving in the Navajo culture.*

❑ *Perform the story as Reader's Theater.*

Using Reader's Theater

After students have read the selection, discuss it with them. Review the different parts of the loom and what they represent to the Navajo. Ask: *What is the important message Spider Woman shares with Changing Woman? How can it be applied, not only to the Navajo but to all peoples?* (Answers may vary)

Have students perform the story as Reader's Theater. Remind students that in a Reader's Theater performance, the actors do not move around the stage, but remain seated and use only their voices as a means to act out the dialog. Choose volunteers to play the roles of Changing Woman, Monster Slayer, Child Born for Winter and Spider Woman. Another student can read the narration. Students can use dialog from the story and adapt some of the narrative as dialog. The remaining students can make drawings of scenes or characters from the story to be displayed as a backdrop for the reading.

SPANISH PIONEERS OF THE SOUTHWEST
by Joan Anderson
Pages 23–26

Use with Chapter 2, Lesson 3

Objectives

❑ *Recognize how early Spanish settlers lived in the Southwest.*

❑ *Describe how, after working hard on the farm, Miguel celebrated the Feast of San Ysidro (arrival of spring).*

❑ *Write a description of a ceremony.*

Writing About a Ceremony

After students have read the selection, have them discuss life on the Baca family farm in the mid-1700s. Ask them: *What is Pedro Baca worried about?* (His older brother was taken by Navajo in a raid.) Discuss with students the importance of farming for the Baca family. Ask students: *What does Pedro look forward to?* (the Feast of San Ysidro) Discuss why this holiday was important for the Spanish farmers, and how they celebrated it. (It marked the arrival of spring; farmers receive blessings for the land; there was a procession with Saint Ysidro's statue; there was special food; there was a church ceremony.) Ask students how the Bacas felt about their Pueblo Indian neighbors. (shared appreciation and caring for the land) You might wish to record student responses on the chalkboard.

Ask volunteers to describe ceremonies they know about that celebrate a particular season or event. Then have students write a description of a ceremony. Some students may wish to make up their own ceremony. After students have completed their descriptions, ask volunteers to read them aloud in class. Students may wish to illustrate their written descriptions for display in the classroom.

GIT ALONG, LITTLE DOGIES
Cowboy Song
Pages 27–28

Use with Chapter 2, Lesson 4

Objectives

❑ *Understand why cowboys sang songs on cattle drives.*

❑ *Write a new verse to the song "Git Along, Little Dogies."*

Writing a Song Verse

After students have read the lyrics, tell them that the song is a traditional one with many variations. Discuss with students why cowboys might have sung on the cattle drives. (to pass the time, to entertain themselves) Remind students that cowboys worked day after day, eating and sleeping outdoors. Ask students what the word "dogies" refers to in the song. (motherless or stray calves) Ask: *Why do you think the cowboys sometimes sang to the cattle and the dogies?* (as a way of talking to them)

Have students write a fourth verse to the song. Remind students to try to use rhyming words at the ends of the second and fourth lines. When students have completed their verses, have them draw accompanying illustrations. Encourage volunteers to share their verses and illustrations with the class.

WHEN I WAS YOUNG IN THE MOUNTAINS

by Cynthia Rylant
Pages 30–32

Use with Chapter 3, Lesson 1

Objectives

❑ *Identify some of Cynthia Rylant's memories of living in the mountains.*

❑ *Describe how the use of repetition affects the story.*

❑ *Write a story about everyday life.*

Writing Your Own Story

After students have read the selection, discuss with them the things that the author remembered about her everyday life as a child in the mountains. Have volunteers read aloud their favorite paragraphs from the selection. Then ask volunteers to tell about everyday things that were special to them when they were younger. Encourage students to think about their everyday lives and to compare them with the author's childhood memories.

Have students write a story called *When I Was Young in _____*. Suggest that students begin each paragraph with the phrase, "When I was young in _____." After students have completed their stories, invite volunteers to read them to the class.

THE EVERGLADES, BUFFALO TIGER AND THE RIVER OF GRASS

by Peter Lourie
Pages 33–34

Use with Chapter 3, Lesson 1

Objectives

❑ *Understand how the Everglades have been changed by human interference.*

❑ *Conduct a press conference with Peter Lourie and Buffalo Tiger.*

Conducting a Press Conference

After students have read the selection, discuss it with them. Encourage them to identify how the ecology of the Everglades has changed because of human interference. (Possible responses include: Trees have been cut down; too much hunting of alligators) Then ask: *Who is Buffalo Tiger?* (a Miccosukee Indian, born and raised in the Everglades) *How has his life changed since his boyhood?* (he can no longer make canoes because there are very few trees; there is too much hunting; most of the land is privately owned)

Ask small groups of students to role-play a press conference in which reporters interview the author of this selection and his guide, Buffalo Tiger. Have the group do additional research about the Everglades in an encyclopedia or on the Internet. The student reporters should prepare questions based on this research and the information in the selection. The questions will be answered by the students playing the roles of Peter Lourie and Buffalo Tiger. Have volunteers present their press conference in class.

KNOXVILLE, TENNESSEE

by Nikki Giovanni

Page 35

Use with Chapter 3, Lesson 2

Objectives

- ❑ *Recognize the reasons that the poet likes summer best of all the seasons.*
- ❑ *Identify how Nikki Giovanni uses poetry to describe what summer means to her.*
- ❑ *Write a poem about one of the seasons.*

Writing Your Own Poem

After students have read the poem, discuss with them why they think Nikki Giovanni chose to write a poem about the summer. Have students suppose that the poem had no title. Ask students: *What elements from the poem might help you determine which region the poem is written about?* (fresh corn, okra, gospel music, mountains, warm climate year-round) Ask volunteers to tell which seasons are most special to them. Ask questions such as: *What do you like to do during your favorite season? How does the geography of our region affect the activities you do during each season?*

Then have students write poems about their favorite seasons and illustrate them. Make a bulletin-board display of the poems around the title "Our Favorite Seasons."

JOHN GREENHOW'S STORE

by Ron and Nancy Goor

Pages 36–37

Use with Chapter 4, Lesson 2

Objectives

- ❑ *Identify the ways colonists in Virginia paid for their goods.*
- ❑ *List and discuss items for sale in a general store in colonial Williamsburg.*
- ❑ *Write a response to the question "How was shopping in colonial times similar to and different from shopping today?"*

Linking to Today

After students have read the selection, discuss the methods of buying and selling in colonial Virginia. Ask students: *How did colonists in Virginia pay for goods?* (ready money—Spanish or Dutch coins; notes of credit; barter) *What forms of payment were accepted in John Greenhow's store?* (ready money only) *Why couldn't colonists mint their own money?* (England would not allow it.) Have students look at the photograph of the store and name some of the goods for sale.

Then ask students to compare items available in Greenhow's store to items for sale in a store today. (Responses will vary but may include that many small stores today are more specialized.) Ask students what they think of as a "general store" today. (Accept all reasonable answers.) Have students write a short essay in response to the question "How was shopping in colonial times similar to and different from shopping today?" As a prewriting warm-up, students can make a list or Venn diagram of similarities and differences. When students have finished their essays, ask volunteers to read theirs to the class.

BATTLE CRY OF FREEDOM
Civil War Battle Song
Pages 38–39

Use with Chapter 4, Lesson 4

Objectives

- ❏ *Identify the perspective revealed in the lyrics to the Northern version of the popular Civil War song "Battle Cry of Freedom."*
- ❏ *Identify the perspective revealed in the lyrics to the Southern version of "Battle Cry of Freedom."*
- ❏ *Write an essay about the different perspectives of the North and the South during the Civil War.*

Exploring Perspectives

After students have read the lyrics, ask volunteers to describe how the songs are alike. (same melody and harmony) Ask students: *How are they different?* (different lyrics) Have students find differences in the lyrics. (Union/Dixie; up with the star/up with the cross; and although he may be poor he shall never be a slave/their motto is resistance—"To tyrants we'll not yield!") Discuss the differences between the North and the South as expressed in the songs.

Have students write a short essay on the different perspectives that the people of the North and the people of the South had during the Civil War. After students have completed their essays, ask volunteers to read them to the class.

ROSA PARKS: MY STORY
by Rosa Parks
Pages 40–42

Use with Chapter 4, Lesson 5

Objectives

- ❏ *Recognize the importance of Rosa Parks's refusal to give up her seat on a bus.*
- ❏ *Identify how reading Rosa Parks's own words helps to better understand the event.*
- ❏ *Write a newspaper article about the event described in Rosa Parks: My Story.*

Rewriting in Another Genre

After students have read the excerpt from *Rosa Parks: My Story*, have volunteers read the selection aloud. Ask students to identify the parts of the story that only Rosas Parks knows. (the many places where she describes her thoughts and feelings) Ask students why Rosa Parks finally wrote her own story about the events of December 1955. (probably to finally tell the details correctly)

Have students rewrite *Rosa Parks: My Story* as a newspaper article. Remind students of the "5 Ws"—the *who, what, when, where,* and *why.* Suggest that in their articles students "interview" the bus driver and other passengers on the bus. After students have completed their articles, ask volunteers to read them to the rest of the class.

FALL

by Karla Kuskin

Page 44

Use with Chapter 5, Lesson 2

Objectives

- ❑ *Identify images of autumn in the Northeast in Karla Kuskin's poem "Fall."*
- ❑ *Write a poem about another season.*

Writing a Poem

After students have read the poem, ask volunteers to read it aloud. Have students describe some of the sensory images the poet uses. (Students might quote such lines as "The black bears roar like thunder," or "I crunch through piles of . . . leaves.") Ask students: *If you could not see the title or first line, which parts of the poem would help you to determine which season the poem is about?* (chipmunks gathering butternuts, colorful hat and jacket, red and yellow leaves) *How does the time of year and climate affect people's activities?* (Answers will vary.)

After the group discussion have students write a poem about one of the other seasons of the year. Ask them to think about distinguishing characteristics of the seasons and have them include these elements in their poems. Have volunteers read their poems to the class.

BLOW, YE WINDS, IN THE MORNING

Pages 45–46

Use with Chapter 5, lesson 3

Objectives

- ❑ *Explain why the Northeast was a rich whaling area.*
- ❑ *Identify how the song "Blow, Ye Winds, in the Morning" describes aspects of the whaling industry.*
- ❑ *Write additional verses to "Blow, Ye Winds, in the Morning."*

Writing Your Own Song Verse

After students have read the lyrics, discuss with students why sailors might have made up such a song. (to pass time and amuse themselves on long trips) Have students identify other things mentioned in the song associated with the Northeast and the whaling industry. (New Bedford, whaling ports, clipper ships, running gear) Ask students: *What example of exaggeration can you find in this song?* (hunting 500 whales in six months) *Why do you think the whalers exaggerated?* (to get sailors to work on their ships)

Divide the class into small groups and have each group write one new verse to the song. Encourage students to think of experiences whalers might have while harvesting the sea. Remind students to pay attention to the use of exaggeration and the repetition of the words *out—singin'* in the verses' fourth lines. After the verses have been completed, copy song sheets for "hearty" classmates to sing and enjoy. The illustrated songs can become part of a sea-theme bulletin board. Students might wish to record their sailing songs.

"WOODPECKER AND SUGAR MAPLE"
retold by Jane Louise Curry
Page 47

Use with Chapter 6, Lesson 1

Objectives
❑ *Recognize that these stories emphasize the importance of mutual dependence in nature.*

❑ *Perform "Woodpecker and Sugar Maple" as Readers Theater.*

Using Readers Theater
After students have read the selection, discuss it with them. Ask students: *How is Woodpecker able to help Sugar Maple?* (by eating the grubs and beetles that are causing him to be uncomfortable). *How is Sugar Maple able to help Woodpecker?* (by telling him to make a hole in his trunk and drink the sweet sap to quench his terrible thirst) *What does this story teach?* (the importance of depending on each other in order to survive, and the specific characteristics that lead to certain behaviors in nature)

Ask students to think of other examples in nature that show how species interact with one another in order to survive. (Answers will vary but might include: trees provide homes to squirrels, birds and other wildlife; the importance of predators, like wolves, in maintaining a valuable part of our ecosystem; lizards, toads and bats eat insects in order to survive and help to limit the number of pests that eat crops)

Have students perform "Woodpecker and Sugar Maple" as Readers Theater. Choose volunteers to play all the roles. Choose another student to act as the narrator. Encourage students to familiarize themselves with their lines before the performance. Students who are not playing roles may wish to make drawings of scenes or characters from the story and use them as part of the setting.

PAUL REVERE'S RIDE
by Henry Wadsworth Longfellow
Pages 48–51

Use with Chapter 6, Lesson 2

Objectives
❑ *Recognize the importance of Paul Revere's ride to the American Revolution.*

❑ *Identify how Longfellow uses language to dramatize the story of Revere's ride.*

❑ *Rewrite the poem as a newspaper article.*

Rewriting in Another Genre
After students have read the poem, invite volunteers to read verses or have the class do a choral reading of the poem. Ask students: *Why was Paul Revere's ride important?* (Because of his warning, Americans had time to prepare for a British attack.) After each section of the poem is read, ask students to summarize the *who, what, when, where,* and *why* of the story. The responses can be recorded on chart paper or on the chalkboard. Encourage students to make notes on these summaries, which they can include in a time line of Revere's ride.

Guide students working individually, in pairs, or in small groups, to rewrite the poem as a newspaper article. First have students review their summaries of the poem's sections. Before they start their newspaper articles, remind students of the "5 Ws"—the *who, what, where, when,* and *why.* After students have completed their articles, ask volunteers to read theirs to the rest of the class.

HARD TIMES AT VALLEY FORGE

by Joseph Martin, 1777–1778
Pages 52–53

Use with Chapter 6, Lesson 2

Objectives

❑ *Describe the hardships faced by the soldiers at Valley Forge as described in Joseph Martin's diary.*

❑ *Identify the reasons that Joseph Martin remained in the army despite the hardships.*

❑ *Rewrite Joseph Martin's diary entry as a newspaper article*

Rewriting in Another Genre

Have students share in reading this selection aloud. After the selection has been read, discuss with students the hardships described by Joseph Martin. (lack of food, water, clothing, and shelter; fatigue; freezing temperatures) Ask students which of Joseph Martin's experiences they consider to have been the most difficult. Have students look again at the selection to find a sentence in his diary that explains why Martin may have been willing to undergo such extreme hardship. (Martin wrote: "We had engaged in the defense of our injured country and were willing, nay, we were determined to persevere as long as such hardships were not altogether intolerable. . . . ") Ask students why Joseph Martin might have decided to keep a diary during this difficult experience. (to stave off boredom, to relieve loneliness, to help him remember the period in his life after the war was over)

Have students rewrite *Hard Times at Valley Forge* as a newspaper article. Remind students of the "5 Ws"—the *who, what, when, where,* and *why.* After students have completed their articles, have volunteers read them aloud to the class.

THE MEMORY COAT

by Elvira Woodruff
Pages 54–55

Use with Chapter 6, Lesson 3

Objectives

❑ *Identify the problems faced by immigrants coming to America in the early 1900s.*

❑ *Understand the relationships between story characters.*

❑ *Perform scenes from the story "The Memory Coat."*

Performing Dramatic Scenes

After students have read the selection, encourage them to discuss the problems faced by immigrants coming to America in the early 1900s. Ask them: *Why does Rachel and Grisha's family decide to leave Russia to come to America?* (It was no longer safe for them in their native country. They feared the Cossacks would kill them because they were Jewish.) Encourage students to discuss the relationships among the characters. Ask: *Based on their words and actions, how do Rachel and Grisha feel about one another?* (Answers may vary; however students should note that the cousins are extremely close. They have invented their own story telling game which Rachel uses to comfort Grisha. Rachel understands that Grisha wants to keep his old coat because it reminds him of his mother. Rachel comes up with a plan so her cousin can pass the inspection at Ellis Island.)

Begin by brainstorming a list of scenes from the story with the students. Then divide the class into small groups. Ask each group to choose one of the scenes to present in class. Different students can volunteer to be directors, actors, stage managers, and prop people. Students should use the dialog from the story, however, they can make up additional dialog as well. One of the student actors can read the story narrative. After they have rehearsed their scenes, call on different groups to perform them in class.

THE BIG RIVERS
by Bruce Hiscock
Pages 57–58

Use with Chapter 7, Lesson 1

Objectives

- ❏ *Understand how the disruption of the normal weather pattern caused the flood.*
- ❏ *Discuss how people responded to the flood.*
- ❏ *Role play an interview with someone who lived or worked in the area affected by the flood of 1993.*

Role-Playing an Interview

After students have read the selection, ask them to identify the three stages in the water cycle. List responses on chart paper or the chalkboard. (evaporation: the sun's energy changes water into water vapor; condensation: as water vapor rises, it cools and changes back into clouds; precipitation: cloud water falls to Earth as rain, snow, sleet, or hail). Ask students: *How did the normal weather patterns in the Midwest change in 1993 and contribute to the Great Flood?* (Humid air that was full of moisture from the Gulf of Mexico flowed north. It created thunderstorms as it clashed with cool air from Canada. These thunderstorms stalled over Iowa, Missouri, and neighboring states, drenching the area and causing flooding.) *What did people in the affected communities do to save their land?* (They built dams of sandbags. Everyone volunteered. National Guard troops and prison crews joined the effort. Restaurants donated food; companies donated bottled water.)

Remind students that the author interviewed people who lived in the flooded area as part of his research. Have pairs of students role play an interview between a newspaper or television reporter and one of the volunteers who is making sandbags during the flood. Before planning the interview, ask students to do additional research about the flood of 1993, using encyclopedias or Internet resources. After students have rehearsed their interviews, call on volunteers to present their role-plays in class. If a videocamera is available, tape the presentations and replay them for the class.

BRINGING THE PRAIRIE HOME
by Patricia MacLachlan
Pages 59–60

Use with Chapter 7, Lesson 1

Objectives

- ❏ *Recognize that people's lives are influenced by geography.*
- ❏ *Identify why geographical place is important to Patricia MacLachlan.*
- ❏ *Write a diary entry about the place where you live.*

Writing a Dairy Entry

After students have read the selection, ask them to describe how the author uses different senses to record her impressions of the prairie. (Responses may include that MacLachlan mentions the smell of the earth, the softness of flowers, the look of the skies.) Discuss with students how the prairie has influenced MacLachlan's life. (It gave her a sense of connecting with history. It made her think of the people who lived before her and would live after her.) Ask students: *How did MacLachlan decide to leave clues about herself?* (She wrote in a diary.) *What did MacLachlan carry with her to remind her of the place that changed her?* (a bag of prairie dirt) Discuss with students what happened when MacLachlan took a bag of prairie dirt to a fourth-grade class. (She discovered that the children also had strong feelings about place.)

Ask students to identify the geographical features of the place where they live. Volunteers may give examples of why the place where they live is important to them. Then guide students in writing a diary entry about their "place." Encourage students to use sensory details in their diary entries. You may also wish to ask students to bring in or draw an object that reminds them of their geographical place.

HEARTLAND
by Diane Siebert
Pages 61–64

Use with Chapter 7, Lesson 1

Objectives

- ❏ *Recognize why Diane Siebert calls the Middle West the "heartland."*
- ❏ *Identify how Diane Siebert uses poetry to celebrate the farmers and their land.*
- ❏ *Write a poem about your own region.*

Writing Your Own Poem

After students have read the poem, ask volunteers to read it aloud. Discuss with students why they think that Diane Siebert uses the word *heartland* to describe the Middle West. (because the region produces much of the food that feeds the people of the United States; because the Middle West is geographically at the center of, or at the heart of, the United States; because the heart feeds blood to the body.) Have students imagine that the poem has no title. Ask students: *How would you identify the region that this poem describes?* (fields of grain, blizzards, giant mills, stockyards, wheat fields, cornfields, and the many references to farms and farmers) Have volunteers share features of their own region that make it special. Encourage students to brainstorm about their region. As students name examples, list them on chart paper or on the chalkboard.

Have each student write a poem about his or her region. Encourage students to think about the entire region and the changes that occur with the different seasons of the year. After students have completed their poems, have them draw illustrations to accompany them. Encourage volunteers to share their poems and illustrations with the class.

A BOY NAMED ABE
by Susan Nanus
Pages 65–73

Use with Chapter 8, Lesson 1

Objectives

- ❏ *Identify the strengths Abe Lincoln demonstrated as a boy growing up in Kentucky.*
- ❏ *Describe how scenes in the play A Boy named Abe show those strengths.*
- ❏ *Write an additional scene for the play.*

Writing Your Own Scene

After students have taken turns reading the play aloud, ask them to tell what they have learned about the character of Lincoln as a young boy growing up in Kentucky. (Responses might include comments about Abe's love of reading and how reading helped him; his hardworking and honest nature; his qualities of common sense, determination, and sense of humor.) You may wish to have students perform some scenes or all of the play.

Divide the class into four or five groups. Guide each group to do research in the library to find additional information about young Lincoln that could be the basis for a short scene. Suggest to students that they try to incorporate references to the woods, rivers, and other geographical features of Kentucky in their scenery. Have each group write a scene and read or perform it in the classroom.

GOING HOME TO NICODEMUS
by Daniel Chu and Bill Shaw
Pages 74–77

Use with Chapter 8, Lesson 1

Objectives

❑ *Recognize why, in 1878, freed blacks from Kentucky expected Kansas to be a "Promised Land."*

❑ *Describe what the freed black homesteaders really found in Nicodemus, Kansas.*

❑ *Create a mural showing the expectations, initial disappointment, and fulfilled dreams of the black homesteaders in Kansas.*

Creating a Mural

After students have read the selection, discuss with them the expectations the freed black homesteaders in Kentucky had about traveling to Kansas. (After years of slavery, they were thrilled about the possibility of owning their own land and living as free people.) Have students describe the hardships the members of Reverend Hickman's church endured on their journey to Kansas. Then ask students: *What did the freed men and women actually find in Nicodemus, Kansas?* (Instead of a Promised Land they found settlers living in holes in the ground.) Discuss with students how the black homesteaders took their deep disappointment. (Many stayed on, and with great faith, built up Nicodemus as a thriving all-black frontier town in the Great Plains.)

Divide students into three groups covering these phases: freed black homesteaders' hard journey to Kansas, looking forward to the Promised Land; their disappointment on finding a desolate area without any comforts; and the all-black frontier town years later, with businesses, schools, and places of worship and recreation. Guide the three groups to create a three-part mural with the title "The Pioneering Spirit: Going Home to Nicodemus."

Students might enjoy reading all of *Going Home to Nicodemus*, which they may be able to find in their school or local library.

THE BUFFALO GO
by Old Lady Horse
Pages 78–79

Use with Chapter 8, Lesson 2

Objectives

❑ *Recognize how the legend makes clear the importance of the buffalo to the Kiowa.*

❑ *Compare and contrast the perspectives of the Kiowa and the hunters.*

Exploring Perspectives

After students have read the legend, discuss it with them. Ask volunteers to describe the reasons that the buffalo were important to the Kiowa. (They were sacrificed in the Sun Dance and used in the Kiowa's prayers; hides were used to make clothing and tepees; meat was used for food; bladders and stomachs were made into containers.) Ask students: *How did the buffalo become nearly extinct?* (Too many were killed.) *Why did some white settlers kill the buffalo?* (to make room for railroads, farms, and ranches; to sell the hides; to force the Indians onto reservations)

Have students discuss the different perspectives of the Kiowa and some white settlers toward the buffalo. Ask students: *Do you think that the perspective of the white hunters might be different today?* (Probably; because today there is more understanding and respect for other cultures.)

Have students write a short essay on the different perspectives of the Kiowa and some white settlers during the late 1800s. After students have completed their essays, ask volunteers to read them aloud.

HITTING THE ROAD
Automobile Advertisements, 1902 and 1924
Page 80

Use with Chapter 8, Lesson 3

Objectives

- ❑ *Compare automobile advertisements.*
- ❑ *Create a poster for a new product that will improve people's lives.*

Creating a Poster

After students have read the introductory material, discuss the information with them. Then guide students to look at the advertisements and discuss why these products would have appealed to their intended audience. (The automobile created more jobs and provided a quicker and easier form of transportation.) Ask students what they like and dislike about the automobiles in the advertisements.

Have students create a poster showing an advertisement for a product of their choice. Suggest students show an ad for today on the left side of the poster. On the right side of the poster, have students draw an ad for the future. Ask them to write advertising copy describing the product. Display the completed advertisements on the bulletin board.

WORKING THE LAND
by Pierce Walker
Pages 81–82

Use with Chapter 8, Lesson 4

Objectives

- ❑ *Describe the life of Pierce Walker working on Indiana farms.*
- ❑ *Identify how farm life in Indiana has changed for Walker through the years.*
- ❑ *Write questions to ask in an interview with a farmer.*

Writing an Interview

After students have read the selection, discuss it with them. Ask why Walker thinks farming is such a gamble and hard work. (dependence on weather, rising prices, long hours) Ask students: *What are some of the changes in farming Walker has experienced over the years?* (farming becoming big business; management problems; changing technology) Ask students: *If working on a farm is so hard for Walker and his family, why have they continued to farm?* (the pride of producing good crops, pride in work, often good to be by yourself in the fields)

If possible, arrange to visit a farm or have a farmer visit the class. Have students work in pairs to write questions for the interview. Guide one student in each pair to write down the question; the other student, the answer. Gather the questions and answers in a class book called "Working the Land." You might wish to have groups illustrate the cover and inside contents.

LEGENDS OF LANDFORMS, "MATEO TEEPEE"

A Cheyenne Legend, retold by Carole G. Vogel
Page 84

Use with Chapter 9, Lesson 1

Objectives

❑ *Understand how legends try to explain natural events.*

❑ *Identify what legends teach about the culture of a people.*

❑ *Write a poem about Mateo Teepee.*

Writing Your Own Poem

After students have read the selection, discuss it with them. Ask students to describe the natural occurrence this legend explains. (It explains the origin of Mateo Teepee, a huge shaft of bare rock in Wyoming.) Ask students: *Why do you think the Cheyenne people wanted to explain how this great rock was formed?* (Possible responses: The rock fascinated them because of its great size and unusual markings.) *How would you compare the legend with a scientific explanation?* (Answers may vary. Possible response: The legend is more imaginative. The scientific explanation is factual.) Then point out that reading legends is one way we can learn more about the culture of an ancient people. Encourage students to discuss what they learned about the Cheyenne culture by reading this legend. (Possible response: The safety of their children was very important to the parents. Men hunted while women prepared meals. They believed in spirits who helped them escape danger. They were cautious in unfamiliar surroundings.)

Have students discuss their thoughts about the legend and the scientific explanation for Mateo Teepee. Encourage them to find a picture of this famous rock in an encyclopedia or by using an on-line reference. Then, ask them to write a poem about this natural phenomenon and to draw pictures to accompany their writing. Their poem can be descriptive, or it can tell a story. Encourage students to share their poems in small groups. Display their poems and drawings on a classroom bulletin board.

ONCE A WOLF

by Stephen R. Swinburne
Pages 85–86

Use with Chapter 9, Lesson 1

Objectives

❑ *Recognize the importance of wolves as predators in nature and their significant contribution to a delicate ecosystem.*

❑ *Identify how living things interact.*

❑ *Identify and research an ecosystem.*

Researching an Ecosystem

After students have read the selection, discuss it with them. Ask students to describe some of their opinions about wolves. *Where did their opinions originate?* (Answers will vary.) *How have their opinions changed after reading the selection?* (Answers will vary.) *Why is it important for wolves to inhabit their natural environs?* (they are predators and important in maintaining the delicate balance of their ecosystem.)

Divide the class into five groups. Have each group choose one kind of ecosystem and research a plant or animal that lives there. Some ecosystems they may research are the desert, tropical rain forest, freshwater rivers, saltwater shores, open sea—surface or deeper down, and forest lands. Have each group draw a labeled illustration that shows how the organism interacts with its surroundings. Ask each group to present their illustrations to the class and explain how their plant or animal survives in its environment.

OFF THE MAP: THE JOURNALS OF LEWIS AND CLARK
edited by Peter and Connie Roop
Page 87

Use with Chapter 10, Lesson 2

Objectives

❏ *Appreciate the rigors involved in Lewis and Clark's exploration of western North America.*

❏ *Trace their route to the headwaters of the Missouri River.*

Background Information

Merriwether Lewis began his epic journey in July 1803 by traveling overland from Washington D.C., to Pittsburgh. From there he boarded a boat headed down the Ohio River and picked up William Clark and others at Louisville, Kentucky. The little group continued on to the point where the Mississippi and Ohio rivers converge. From there they headed up the Mississippi to St. Louis to a trading post, which was founded by the French near where the Missouri flows into the Mississippi. There they stayed for five months in order to prepare for the hardest part of their journey. In May 1804 the Lewis and Clark expedition to the Pacific Northwest began in earnest.

Tracing a Route

Divide the class into groups. Assign to each group a section of Lewis and Clark's route. Have each group trace their section of the route from an atlas map. (Note: the group didn't immediately hook up with the present-day Columbia River; they followed the present-day Lemhi, Salmon, and Snake rivers to the Columbia.) Have them note which states the expedition traveled through as well as the type of terrain they encountered along the way. Have each group share their findings with the rest of the class.

DOTY'S WASHER
Advertisement from the 1800s
Page 88

Use with Chapter 10, Lesson 2

Objectives

❏ *Recognize why housekeepers in the 1800s would prefer Doty's Washer to the old washboard.*

❏ *Create a poster for a new product that will improve people's lives.*

Creating a Poster

Ask students to read the introductory material and discuss the information with them. Guide students to look at the poster and discuss why the washer might appeal to housekeepers in the 1800s. (Doty's Washer promised to save them time as well as wear and tear on their clothes.) Have students discuss what they like and dislike about the washer. Ask them how it compares to modern day washing machines.

Have students create a poster showing an advertisement for a product of their choice. On the left side have them show how the product looks today. On the right side, ask them to draw the same product as it might look in the future with different improvements made to it. Ask students to write advertising copy describing the product. Display the completed posters in the classroom.

WAITING ON WYOMING
by Navidad O'Neill
Pages 89–96

Use with Chapter 10, Lesson 3

Objectives

❑ *Recognize why the territory of Wyoming was important in the women's suffrage movement in 1869.*

❑ *List the reasons people were for and against women voting in Wyoming.*

❑ *Perform the play Waiting on Wyoming.*

Performing a Play

After students have read the play, discuss it with them. Ask students why the territory of Wyoming is important in the history of the women's suffrage movement. (In 1869 Wyoming allowed women to vote in its elections—the first place in this country where women could do so.) Have students list the reasons people were for and against women voting. (For example, *for:* women should have same rights as men; *against:* women will become like men.) Have students brainstorm ideas on how they can perform the play; for example, who will play the characters, what costumes and props can be used, where the play will be set, and so on.

After the brainstorming session, divide the class into three groups: students who volunteer to be the student director, stage manager, and prop people; students who will play the characters from Wyoming; and students who will play the chorus of newspaper editors back East. List on the chalkboard the names of students playing the characters (stage managers can keep a record, too). With student directors and stage managers, work out the play's blocking and movement. Lay out a rehearsal schedule and decide on simple scenery (colorful signs) and costumes (for example, long skirts for girls) to show place and time. Form costume and prop committees. Make sure students know their lines before performing the play.

SIERRA
by Diane Siebert
Pages 98–101

Use with Chapter 11, Lesson 1

Objectives

❑ *Recognize how Diane Siebert uses poetry to describe the history of the Sierra Mountains.*

❑ *Recognize some of the changes in the history of the Sierra Mountains.*

❑ *Write a letter to Diane Siebert.*

Writing a Letter

After students have read the poem silently, ask volunteers to read the poem aloud. Discuss with students why Diane Siebert might have chosen to write a poem about the Sierras. Point out to students that Siebert describes changes that have taken place in the mountains over millions of years. Ask students to skim the poem to find some of these changes. Then ask a volunteer to read the last stanza of the poem. Discuss with students the meaning of Siebert's warning that the mountains depend on how people care for them.

Have students write a letter to Diane Siebert describing how people can take care of the mountains. After students have completed their letters, have volunteers read theirs to the class. Encourage students to mail their letters to Siebert.

THE YEAR OF MISS AGNES
by Kirkpatrick Hill
Pages 102–103

Use with Chapter 11, Lesson 1

Objectives

❑ *Recognize the importance of the student/teacher relationship in the story.*

❑ *Identify on a map the geographic locations discussed in the story.*

❑ *Link the Alaskan students' experience of education in 1948 to the experience of students today.*

Linking to Today

After students have read the selection, have them discuss the characters' perspectives about their environment. Ask: *Why is learning important to them?* (reading and arithmetic are important to know so they can conduct business in the real world and not be taken advantage of; learning about the world outside of their small village broadens their perspectives) *Although the story takes place about 55 years ago, are the characters' needs and wants much different from the needs and wants of students today?* (Answers will vary.) *How would you describe the relationship between Miss Agnes and her students?* (respectful, caring, honest) Ask students if they have ever visited Alaska or other parts of the United States, or have gone to the home of a family that follows different traditions or practices. Have volunteers share what it was like for them to experience new things or unfamiliar places.

Challenge students to think about aspects of American culture that would be new and interesting to the Athabascan children of Alaska. If there are students in the class who are from different societies, ask them to share their impressions of American popular culture. Then have students think about the difficulties they might experience if they and their families moved to a different country or environment.

KAIULANI, THE PEOPLE'S PRINCESS
by Ellen Emerson White
Page 104

Use with Chapter 12, Lesson 1

Objectives

❑ *Identify some of Kaiulani's personal strengths.*

❑ *Write an essay about Kaiulani.*

Writing an Essay

After students have read the diary entry, discuss it with the class. Ask students to share their reactions to Kaiulani and her cause. Encourage students to talk about the obstacles in her way. (She was a young girl being undermined by powerful American businessmen.)

Have students reread the selection and write a few sentences that summarize the diary entry. Encourage students to do additional research on the Internet or in reference books. Ask them to use their sentences and research as a guideline for a brief essay on Kaiulani. After students have completed their essays, have volunteers read them to the class.

BY THE GREAT HORN SPOON!
by Sid Fleischman
Pages 105–107

Use with Chapter 12, Lesson 2

Objectives

- ❑ *Recognize why Jack and Praiseworthy went to California during the mid-1800s.*
- ❑ *Recognize some of the hardships of mining camps during the Gold Rush.*
- ❑ *Perform a Reader's Theater of* By the Great Horn Spoon!

Using Readers Theater

After students have read the selection, discuss it with them. Ask students to describe how Jack and Praiseworthy were typical of other Forty-Niners. (They went to California to get rich quick and then leave.) Then ask students what Jack and Praiseworthy had learned by the end of the story. (that getting rich quick was not going to be as easy as they hoped)

Have students perform *By the Great Horn Spoon!* as Reader's Theater. Remind students that in a Reader's Theater performance, the actors do not move around on a stage but remain seated and use only their voices as a means to act out the dialogue. The selection gives students an opportunity to read some interesting vocabulary. Choose students to take the parts of Jack, Praiseworthy, the waiter, the miner, and the narrator. Several students might take the parts of other miners in the camp. Encourage students to familiarize themselves with their lines before the performance.